ROUTLEDGE LIBRARY EDITIONS:
SOUTH AFRICA

Volume 19

THE LIBERAL DILEMMA IN SOUTH AFRICA

THE LIBERAL DILEMMA IN SOUTH AFRICA

Edited by
PIERRE L. VAN DEN BERGHE

LONDON AND NEW YORK

First published in 1979 by Croom Helm Ltd

This edition first published in 2023
by Routledge
4 Park Square, Milton Park, Abingdon, Oxon OX14 4RN

and by Routledge
605 Third Avenue, New York, NY 10158

Routledge is an imprint of the Taylor & Francis Group, an informa business

© 1979 Croom Helm Ltd

All rights reserved. No part of this book may be reprinted or reproduced or utilised in any form or by any electronic, mechanical, or other means, now known or hereafter invented, including photocopying and recording, or in any information storage or retrieval system, without permission in writing from the publishers.

Trademark notice: Product or corporate names may be trademarks or registered trademarks, and are used only for identification and explanation without intent to infringe.

British Library Cataloguing in Publication Data
A catalogue record for this book is available from the British Library

ISBN: 978-1-032-30347-5 (Set)
ISBN: 978-1-032-32213-1 (Volume 19) (hbk)
ISBN: 978-1-032-32219-3 (Volume 19) (pbk)
ISBN: 978-1-003-31343-4 (Volume 19) (ebk)

DOI: 10.4324/9781003313434

Publisher's Note
The publisher has gone to great lengths to ensure the quality of this reprint but points out that some imperfections in the original copies may be apparent.

Disclaimer
The publisher has made every effort to trace copyright holders and would welcome correspondence from those they have been unable to trace.

This is a reissue of a previously published book. The language is reflective of the time in which this book was published. In reissuing this book, no offence is intended by the Publishers to any reader.

THE LIBERAL DILEMMA IN SOUTH AFRICA
Edited by Pierre L. van den Berghe

CROOM HELM LONDON

© 1979 Pierre L. van den Berghe
Croom Helm Ltd, 2-10 St John's Road, London SW11

British Library Cataloguing in Publication Data

The liberal dilemma in South Africa.
   1. South Africa – Politics and government –
   1961- 2. Liberalism – South Africa
   I. Van den Berghe, Pierre Louis
   320.5'1'0968   JQ1915

ISBN 0-7099-0136-4

Printed in Great Britain by
Biddles Ltd, Guildford, Surrey

CONTENTS

1. Introduction *Pierre L. van den Berghe* — 7
2. Predicaments and Options of Critical Intellectuals at South African Universities
   Heribert Adam — 17
3. Commitment: the Liberal as Scholar in South Africa
   Hilda Kuper — 30
4. On the Liberal Definition of the South African Situation
   Hamish Dickie-Clark — 48
5. The Impossibility of a Liberal Solution in South Africa
   Pierre L. van den Berghe — 56
6. Sociology and Universal Reality: South African Implications
   Fatima Meer — 68
7. The Magician and the Missionary
   Adam Kuper — 77
8. The African Doctor: his Role in the Community
   Hilstan L. Watts — 97
9. The Political Implications of a Split Labour Market Analysis of South African Race Relations
   Edna Bonacich — 106
10. The Politicisation of Ethnic Universities: Experiences with South Africa's 'College Brews'
    Kogila A. Moodley — 117
11. Intellectuals and Academic Apartheid, 1950-1965
    Margo Russell — 133
12. Biographic Sketch and Bibliography of Leo Kuper — 153

Notes on Contributors — 157

Index — 159

THE LIBERAL DILEMMA IN SOUTH AFRICA

1 INTRODUCTION

Pierre L. van den Berghe

In a conflict-ridden society such as South Africa both the stridency and the relevance of ideology are inevitably heightened. South Africa grew out of a colonial slave society, and its ruling class gradually developed an articulated ideology to justify its domination. A unique blend of Calvinist predestination, racism, paternalism, Old Testament patriarchalism, and nationalism, this legitimating ideology became increasingly explicit and eventually grew into a full-blown model for perpetuating minority rule in a plural society. Called apartheid in 1948, it was later relabelled 'separate development' when the word 'apartheid' became unsavoury, even to those previously its advocates.

Every thesis calls forth its antithesis. South Africa, being the extraordinarily complex society that it is, has produced three antitheses to apartheid. To simplify, we may label them 'black nationalism,' 'liberalism,' and 'Marxism.' Since apartheid and Afrikaner nationalism are ideologies of white domination, one obvious, and probably the most elemental, response is black nationalism. Black nationalism in its extreme form may become as racist as its white counterpart, but it has not generally become so in South Africa. In fact, it has mostly been quite subdued, and even recent manifestations of it tend to softpedal racist undertones. However, as the conflict becomes increasingly exacerbated, the likelihood of racial polarisation, and hence the chances of black nationalism, are clearly increasing.

The great moral alibi of black nationalism, not only in South Africa, but elsewhere on the continent as well, has been the liberal principle of majority rule. If your constituency has the good fortune to contain a demographic majority, racism can easily be disguised as domocracy. The ideological sleight of hand, of course, is that an ascriptive, racially-defined majority is a far cry from a majority made up of shifting coalitions of individuals on the basis of commonality of beliefs and interests. 'Majority rule' in Africa can thus easily become a liberal veneer for racial domination.

Liberalism is another antithesis to apartheid. Apartheid is premised on preserving and constructing barriers between racial and ethnic groups, in treating people first and foremost as members of racial and ethnic groups, and in using those carefully nurtured group differences as bases of differential and unequal treatment by the state, which thus becomes the instrument of domination by one racial group. Liberalism, by contrast, adamantly rejects all forms of state recognition of groups and advocates incorporation of citizens into the state as individuals on the basis of equality of rights (subject to qualifications of age, mental competence, good behavior, and until recently, sex).

South African liberalism sometimes traces back its ancestry to the 'Cape Liberalism' of the nineteenth century, but while Cape Liberalism bore some of the trademarks of its British origins, it quickly acquired a heavy dosage of colonial paternalism when it took root in South African soil. In the twentieth century, South African liberalism took over Gandhist and Fabian socialist elements which again gave it a distinctive flavour, and made it very different from 'Cape Liberalism'. The heyday of South African liberalism (such as it was, for it never had any mass appeal) probably was during the two post-World-War-II decades. Much of the content of this book deals with that epoch. The events of the last fifteen years or so are making liberalism increasingly irrelevant and unlikely to provide a solution to South Africa's problems. This book is thus an epitaph. Liberalism failed in South Africa; it failed nobly, for complex reasons which had little to do with its proponents, but it failed all the same.

Finally, there is the Marxist antithesis to apartheid. Apartheid attributes prime importance to racial and ethnic affiliation and erects a society committed to the maintenance of ascriptive barriers and differential treatment. Marxism attributes near-exclusive importance to class, and treats ethnic and racial divisions as derivative of relations of production. As an ideology, it advocates a society in which both class, and racial or ethnic distinctions would be abolished or become irrelevant. The Marxist antithesis shares with liberalism an adamant opposition to all racial and ethnic discrimination, and hence to the entire apparatus of apartheid. However, through identification of blacks with the revolutionary proletariat, Marxists have found it quite easy to establish pragmatic alliances with black nationalist movements, frequently building into the revolutionary scenario a temporarily progressive role for the 'nationalist bourgeoisie'. The main strains of the South African revolutionary movement are based on such a pragmatic alliance.

The contributors to this collection share two broad characteristics. They are intellectuals — for the most part politically committed ones — and they are roughly in the liberal band of the political spectrum. This collection therefore sheds light on two interesting features of South African society: the place of intellectuals and the role of liberalism. I

Introduction

shall discuss each briefly.

Of the vast literature on South Africa, relatively little has been explicitly devoted to the role of intellectuals in that extraordinary society. This is doubly surprising, both because of the relative prominence of intellectuals in public life, and because much penetrating analysis of South Africa has been produced by intellectuals, both foreign and domestic. Yet for a variety of complex reasons, including the deep emotional involvement of scholars in the reality they were studying, and often a sense of futility concerning their efforts, South African intellectuals have been reluctant to indulge in self-analysis. Despite the distinguished tradition of social anthropology, nurtured on South African soil, South Africa has produced no such works as *Tristes Tropiques* or *Return to Laughter*.

What South Africa has produced, however, is an abundant crop of committed intellectuals of all persuasions who were often both acute observers of and active participants in the political, economic, social and artistic life of the country. Many were academics, especially in the social sciences, like Max Gluckman, Isaac Schapera, Archie Mafeje, Leo Kuper, Hilda Kuper, Monica Wilson, Cornelis De Kiewiet, Ralph Horwitz, Julius Lewin, Fatima Meer, E.G. Malherbe, Leonard Thompson, and, of course, H.F. Verwoerd, though most of us are not eager to claim the latter as a colleague. Others were prominent in journalism and letters like Alan Paton, Leo Marquard, Ezekiel Mphahlele, Nadine Gordimer, Bloke Modisane, and Jordan Ngubane. Some were churchmen like Trevor Huddleston, Beyers Naude, Denis Hurley, Joos de Blank, and Ambrose Reeves. Others yet became engulfed in the maelstrom of politics, covering a wide ideological spectrum from Peter Brown, Edgar Brookes, Jack Simons, Helen Suzman, Z.K. Matthews and Albert Luthuli to Jan Smuts. Many have spent time in prison, including distinguished visitors like Mahatma Gandhi, and, increasingly since 1948, hundreds have opted for or been forced into exile.

It may seem paradoxical that in a country so permeated by the insanities of racism, people of intellect should not only have figured so prominently in public affairs, but should have been taken so seriously. True, their warnings and prognoses generally went unheeded, but intellectuals were often taken earnestly enough to warrant harassment, prosecution, imprisonment, banishment, exile, censorship and other repressive measures. Perhaps the greatest compliment paid by the Nationalist government to the power of ideas is that the ruling group enlisted in the defence of the indefensible the ponderous ratiocinations of its academics at Stellenbosch, Potchefstrom and Pretoria, that it created the South African Bureau of Racial Affairs to spin out a tortuously elaborate rationale for apartheid, and that doctrinal hair-splitting between *verligtes* and *verkramptes* makes front-page news in the Nationalist press. Not content merely to rule, the government also seemingly wants to justify itself and be 'understood'. To whom and by whom one wonders.

The nature of the relationship between a society and its intellectual life has not been subjected to much empirical research. It is often assumed that it takes a 'free' society — by which is usually meant a Western liberal democracy such as Holland, Britain or the United States — to experience the fluorescence of intellectual culture. I should like to suggest that the optimum milieu for the development of an active and creative intelligentsia is a grossly unjust and indefensible social order backed up by a moderately and inefficiently repressive regime, under economic conditions that are far from good but securely above the level of starvation, at least for educated urban-dwellers. In a sense, I have also described the ideal conditions for a revolutionary situation. South Africa admirably fits that description; so did Bourbon France, Czarist Russia, colonial India, Ghana and Algeria. Such is the social climate that fosters intellects like Voltaire, Tolstoi, Gandhi, Nkrumah, or Fanon. In a 'free' society such as the United States, their likes are professors of philosophy at Brandeis who experience at best the transient notoriety of intellectual fads. In a ruthlessly repressive society like Nazi Germany or Stalinist Russia, they would not have survived their first adolescent pamphlet. Born as hungry peasants in a desperately poor society, they would have had to use their wits to fill their stomachs, with little time left for revolutionary thinking.

To be sure, there are creative and alienated intellectuals in liberal democracies too, but they typically exert little influence, and, since they risk little except a fleeting popularity among a small coterie, their dissent has little moral weight, and their strictures have the quality of a parlour game engaged in for mutual diversion. They are committed only with the tip of their pen and of their tongue. The Switzerlands and United States of this world cannot produce Dostoievskis and Solzhenitsyns. The Soviet Union and South Africa can and do. This is not to say that most professionals, academics and educated people in these countries have been selfless and courageous intellectuals. Indeed, the vast majority have played it safe. This is hardly surprising when one considers the overwhelming apathy and lack of courage of so many intellectuals even in countries like the United States where the price of dissent is little more than unpopularity and mild social ostracism.

Introduction

Fatima Meer is thus quite justified in attacking the timidity of most of her sociological colleagues in South Africa. The example of people like herself and Leo Kuper who did suffer constant harassment for their openly professed beliefs, and who, within the narrow limits of the possible in a police state, put their beliefs to the constant test of their daily actions, is thus all the more admirable. The remarkable thing, then, is not that there should be so few fearless intellectuals, but that, despite heavy odds, there should be a few hundred or even thousand people who have the courage to be decent in an indecent society.

The reader will not find here a cross-section of South African opinion. If this collection were indeed representative of the country's thinking, South Africa's problems would be largely solved. Alas, only a narrow spectrum of opinion is represented here, which, for lack of a better label, I shall call 'liberal'. The term 'liberal' has been used as a political epithet from both the right and the left, and perhaps not every contributor would be happy to characterise himself as such. Nevertheless, all share a set of fundamental values with the man they honour, and since Leo Kuper was a leading figure in the now defunct South African Liberal Party, the label seems appropriate.

Since systematically entrenched racial discrimination has long been the cornerstone of the present political order in South Africa, one of the central tenets of liberalism (and indeed of the entire Congress movement) in that country is uncompromising opposition to any distinction based on race, colour, creed, or language; the movement also advocates equal political and legal rights for all adults, and recognition on the basis of individual merit and qualities rather than as members of racial or ethnic collectivities. These tenents constitute the common denominator of South African liberalism. In addition to the dismantling of the whole apparatus of apartheid, and the installation of a parliamentary democracy based on universal adult suffrage, many South African liberals, including Leo Kuper and most of the authors of this book, would also welcome a series of social and economic changes consistent with the practices of Western European welfare states, including land reform, nationalisation of means of transport, extractive industries, and public utilities, socialised medicine and welfare services, and free education at all levels including universities. In short, the South African liberal tradition is broadly congruent with the British Fabian Socialist or with the Continental Social Democratic tradition.

It differs, however, from various brands of radical Marxism in two fundamental respects, both of which have been central themes in the scholarly work of Leo Kuper. The first is largely a theoretical disagreement in the analysis of South African society. Marxists tend to reduce all social differences to class, and, thus, to treat race and ethnicity as special cases of class. Leo Kuper has repeatedly argued that class, race and ethnicity are intertwined but analytically distinct bases of social cleavage, and he has demonstrated convincingly that any attempt to reduce everything to class leads to inadequate oversimplifications. Of the contributors to this volume, Edna Bonacich, though not an orthodox Marxist by any standard definition, does defend a class-reductionist view of South African society.

Far more agonising than these fine points of sociological analysis has been the liberals' firm moral rejection of violence as a way of initiating political change. The split with the Marxists, and indeed even with a few radical breakaways within the liberal group, had both an irreconcilable ethical dimension and an arguable tactical basis. These issues were dealt with at length in Leo Kuper's book, *Passive Resistance in South Africa*. To understand the depth of South African liberals' moral commitment to non-violence, one must appreciate the overwhelming imprint of Mahatma Gandhi, not only on the Liberal Party but, more importantly, on the entire Congress movement, which is to say on virtually the entire radical opposition from the 1890s to the early 1960s.

What made commitment to non-violence so difficult to sustain in South Africa was its apparent ineffectiveness as a tactic to bring about social and political change. Even in the case of India, the great success story for *satyagraha*, it is arguable whether independence was the result of Gandhi's campaigns or whether it would have come at approximately the same time as European colonial empires in Asia collapsed in the aftermath of the Second World War. And if *satyagraha* did bring forth independence, it did nothing to prevent the orgy of violence which immediately followed the British withdrawal. In any case, South Africa is not India. The ruling whites are not representatives of a waning colonial empire, but firmly entrenched settlers. To appeal to their sense of human decency has little effect, for their ethos is not one of universalism and fair play, but of racism and *baasskap*.

Satyagraha is, in the last analysis, a persistent moral blackmail; it can only work to the extent that your antagonist shares your values and concedes your moral superiority at the outset. This was the case with the British in India; the principle of Indian self-rule had long been conceded. In South Africa, that fundamental precondition is totally lacking. The government responded to every passive resistance campaign with massive violence. Despite the remarkable courage, discipline and moral

Introduction

stature of the thousands of volunteers in these campaigns, they made little impression beyond a few ripples of temporary disruption. While forms of resistance short of violence against persons, such as strikes, boycotts, and industrial sabotage, can obviously play an important auxiliary role in disrupting the economic and political machinery of the settler state, passive resistance by itself is seemingly incapable of toppling it. Nothing, I fear, short of violent revolution and guerrilla warfare with outside support has realistic prospects of destroying apartheid.

The prognosis for violent change has become increasingly convincing over the years, while the scenarios for evolutionary change seem increasingly implausible. Consequently, moral commitment to non-violence in a situation such as that of South Africa almost inevitably relegates one to the role of a cheering spectator in the revolutionary struggle.

Heribert Adam pleads for realism in our analysis of South Africa, and has taken some of us to task for letting our wishful thinking colour our vision of an unpleasant world. Hilda Kuper reaffirms the theme of the intellectual's involvement in the social 'reality' he observes. Both points are well founded, as these essays (including this introduction) amply demonstrate. As Hilda Kuper puts it, there are situations where ethical neutrality is itself unethical. All of us here feel that racial discrimination in any form is totally indefensible. Therefore, we cannot suspend value judgements when talking about South Africa, nor do we feel that any 'objectivity' is gained by pretending to do so, and hiding our revulsion against apartheid under a coat of academic jargon. It also follows from this stance that we cannot divorce our role as social scientists from our role as critics and ordinary participants in a society.

The man we honour here is a sterling example to us all, for not only is he a leading analyst of apartheid and one of its most articulate critics; his entire life has been dedicated to an active non-violent struggle against it. His role as a leading member of the Liberal Party is well known, but his day to day actions as an academic at the University of Natal deserve mention because they epitomise the stance of the committed intellectual. As Head of the Sociology Department at that institution, he succeeded in running the only academically integrated department in an otherwise racially segregated university. He withstood the strain of police surveillance, knowing that his actions and statements were reported to the government, that his telephone and mail were tampered with, and that his office was searched for incriminating documents. He transferred the entire sociology section of the library from the Main (i.e. white) Library to the vastly inferior branch library of the

'Non-European' campus, so as to make all sociology books equally available to all his students. He refused to hold separate lectures for white and non-white students as other departments were doing, and personally drove his white students to integrated classes on the non-white campus. His department was the only one to have a 'non-white' lecturer, Fatima Meer who, to make matters even more difficult, was also active in the Congress movement. At the same time, the second most senior member of his department was a leading Afrikaner Nationalist. Astonishingly, this very mixed crew managed to get along in a very civilised manner, thanks to this unique blend of gentle even-handedness and passionate commitment to justice that Leo Kuper showed toward us all. Like Mahatma Gandhi, he taught us to hate oppression, not the oppressor.

Leo Kuper's life and works transcend, of course, the narrow confines of South Africa, as the brief biographical sketch shows. After leaving South Africa in 1961, he gladly abandoned the active political arena that was so uncongenial to his temperament. For nothing could have been farther from his ambitions than the pursuit and exercise of power. It took the extreme injustice of South African conditions to bring out the fighter in him. At the University of California at Los Angeles where he continued his distinguished career, Leo Kuper became a leading figure in the rise to prominence of that university's African Studies Center, and turned his own analytical talents to the comparative study of ethnic and racial conflicts and of the bloody turmoil that often results from them. His latest book, *The Pity of It All*, is poignant testimony to the liberal dilemma in South Africa.

The Pity of It All brings us back to South Africa, for it reflects his desperate search for a more humane solution for South Africa. Points of no return are notoriously difficult to establish, except in retrospect. Many anguished voices of warning have passionately pleaded for fundamental change in South Africa as the only means of avoiding catastrophe and massive bloodshed. The predicament of that country is that its ruling albinocracy is so firmly ensconced in its structure of political monopoly and economic privilege that nothing short of an immediate threat will make it change. Such a threat, in turn, only gains credibility when the escalation of violence has already reached a level high enough to make peaceful resolutions all the more difficult.

The root of the South African problem, and the main reason why it is so intractable, is economic. South Africa is still a rather poor, semi-developed country, much better off than India, or Ethiopia, but a long way from Western Europe or even Japan. It is roughly at the level of

Introduction 15

development of such Latin American countries as Mexico or Brazil. But the total dismantling of apartheid with all of its political and economic ramifications which is the *sine qua non* of a just society in South Africa necessarily involves sweeping changes in the economic position of the privileged white group.

Clearly, the South African situation is radically different from the civil rights movement in the United States. The problem is not the assimilation into the mainstream of underprivileged minorities at minimum economic cost to whites, but the abolition of both economic and political privileges of a pampered minority. Unlike in many Latin American countries where social revolution meant the dispossessing of a handful of foreign capitalist enterprises, the Church, and a small oligarchy of a few hundred or thousand landowners, the South African ruling minority is quite large. Unlike in many other former colonial territories where whites were so few that political independence left their economic position largely unaffected, South Africa faces a situation quite similar to Algeria. The abolition of apartheid, even under a conservative, capitalist regime that would merely guarantee legal equality of political rights and of access to economic resources, would inevitably result in a drastic reduction of the standard of living of most whites. Whites would quickly discover that their economic level in a 'free enterprise' system is considerably below their sheltered level under apartheid. The economic position of non-whites would probably improve only marginally, but that of whites would steeply decline, even in the most cautious estimate of what a South African revolution might entail.

If my analysis is correct, it has two corollaries. The first is that neither the present government of South Africa, nor any government that represents the interests of South African whites, can be expected significantly to tamper with the structure of apartheid, except when driven to it by impending defeat, as has happened in the case of the Ian Smith government in Zimbabwe since 1977. The South African government cannot make any real changes without precipitating its own downfall. Its options are to contribute to its own demise through a policy of concessions, or to postpone the day of reckoning by tightening its repressive grip. Naturally, it can be expected to follow the latter course.

The second corollary of my analysis is that, once the level of internal unrest and insurgency and of external sanctions has risen to make South Africa a permanent garrison state with all that implies for the whites, the *dénouement* might be less protracted and less cataclysmic than is often supposed. If, indeed, I am correct in believing that South

African whites are no less rational than other people, and that economic considerations will loom large in their decisions, then most of them can be expected to emigrate. The most likely course of events would be a period of a few years of escalating insurgency supported by outside powers, leading to a flight of foreign and domestic capital, a deterioration of economic conditions, an increasing militarisation of the entire white population, and a growing emigration of whites, starting with the younger and more skilled. The present regime would suffer irreversible erosion from within, until it would collapse with a final rush of whites for the ships and aeroplanes.

This scenario also presupposes, of course, that countries like Australia, New Zealand, Canada, the United States, and Britain would be prepared to absorb the emigrants and sugar coat somewhat the bitter pill of exile. If a small country like Portugal could absorb over half a million people, and if France could take in a million *pieds noirs*, surely four millions would not be an overwhelming burden for Europe, North America and Australia. The likelihood of humanitarian sentiment being mobilised toward that end is rather high, especially as powerful countries like the United States will see support for white emigration as a relatively inexpensive solution to a dangerous problem

Whites should not, of course, be denied the right to live in South Africa on terms of equality with blacks. I, for one, firmly believe that one's skin pigmentation or lack of it should not determine one's claim to live anywhere, or indeed to anything at all. Practically, however, it is doubtful that many whites would want to stay, particularly if that meant a drastically reduced standard of living, as it almost certainly would for at least two-thirds of the white population. Similar populations have not wanted to stay in Algeria, Angola, and Mozambique. There is little ground for assuming that Rhodesians and South Africans will be any different. Length of historical claims, and invocations of depth of roots, make little difference in the crunch. People do, of course, have deep attachments to land, and evolve complex, emotional ideologies around territory; but, in the last analysis, many move to make the most of existing opportunities. It matters little that one's ancestors have been there for 300 or 3000 years. One's future and that of one's children weigh far more heavily in the final balance than the claims of one's ancestors on a piece of turf, however lovely and well-loved. It is simply not true that white South Africans have nowhere else to go, unless the whole world conspires to make it true. That prospect is most unlikely.

2 PREDICAMENTS AND OPTIONS OF CRITICAL INTELLECTUALS AT SOUTH AFRICAN UNIVERSITIES[1]

Heribert Adam

Sociologists frequently remind us that 'institutions are not simply the behaviour and ideas of individuals' (Kuper, 1974, p. 103). While this basic insight must not be overlooked, particularly in the South African context of a widely regulated and politically predetermined institutional structure, the focus of this analysis will be on individual dissent, rather than on the political role of South African universities as institutions. The abstract debate about the political role of universities frequently neglects the fact that its conclusions still depend, among other factors, on the attitudes of university members for their implementation. Max Weber's (1919, 1968) role distinction between the objective, value-neutral scholar inside the classroom and the politically active citizen outside constitutes a laudable ideal type, but is mostly a fiction in reality. In such Weberian terms, this analysis looks at the political roles of South African intellectuals and the content of their beliefs and tactics.

A realistic assessment of the predicaments and options of intellectuals at South African universities under conditions of politically restricted academic freedom and racially determined differential access to educational institutions depends, above all, on a clear understanding of the specific South African scene. The term 'critical intellectual' refers to all those academics — regardless of race, political persuasion and employment, whether at the Afrikaans, black or 'open' English-language universities — who find themselves in substantial disagreement with this set-up, and sincerely desire a radical redistribution of power and wealth in the country as a whole, beyond and different from that envisaged through apartheid. While the equal intellectual skills of the supporters of separate development are not disputed, they are, in accordance with the literature (Gouldner, 1975; Habermas, 1969; Nettl, 1969), assigned the labels intelligentsia, technocrats or ideologues. They fall outside the concern of this analysis.

Unlike the Soviet Union or Nazi Germany, there is no demand for commitment on the part of South African intellectuals, only the expectation of acquiescence and adherence to an increasingly expanding code of undesirable activities. Dissenting academics have no real power to change this situation, but can only make futile, symbolic protests. As individuals, they can be silenced through banning orders; as a group they are dependant on government financing.

On the other hand, there are also several restraining factors for government action: as far as the black universities are concerned, separate development needs the legitimacy of at least partial consent by the subordinates. The goal and necessity for white unity restrains Afrikaner moves against the liberal English-language institutions, which, after all, train scarce white manpower and thereby fulfill a vital service function, too costly for the private sector. In this situation, nominal institutional deviation and even the rhetoric of National Union of South African Students (NUSAS) officials with their overrated following have hardly more than nuisance value which can be tolerated, if periodically checked and intimidated. Unlike in other authoritarian societies, there is still considerable tolerance of dissent in South Africa, and despite the disreputed image overseas, sanctions against individual scholars have been fewer than usually assumed. Furthermore less risks are involved for the intellectual deviant than in Eastern Europe and most African and Asian countries.

How do dissenting intellectuals respond to this situation, in which there is also a much more palpable, universally endorsed cause than the university protest movement in other countries ever had? There seem to be six possible, partly overlapping reactions which can be described as (1) privatism, (2) exile, (3) liberal retreat, (4) militant-radical stance, (5) change through association, (6) political reformism. An attempt will be made to describe and assess these six reactions in terms of (a) their critical content, (b) their likely effectiveness in contributing to a shift in the power hierarchy in South Africa towards a more egalitarian, non-racial society and (c) their impact on South African universities. Analogies could be drawn with intellectuals in other South African institutions, such as the press or the churches, but the focus here is on the crystallisation of dissent in the universities.

Privatism

By far the most common response to the overwhelming power of the state, evidenced in a widespread feeling of paralysis and perceived lack of realistic alternatives, has been an attitude best described as privatism. It does not manifest itself in political disinterest, but may take various forms from cynicism to an 'attitude of detached, urbane amusement at the insanity of Apartheid' (van den Berghe, 1967, p. 170). Its effect is withdrawal into the private realm with neither direct nor indirect involvement in efforts to restore sanity. As such, privatism has conservative implications insofar as it leaves the *status quo* unchallenged.

A prevalent form of this withdrawal among South African academics seems the selection of safe research and noncontroversial teaching. Some of the brightest graduate students are given esoteric historical dissertation topics in the social sciences, while several sociologists agree that 'the discipline had substantially avoided the study of race relations' (Welsh, 1975, p. 28). No doubt, the amply documented (ibid.) though often exaggerated obstacles to free research play a pragmatic part in this self-censorship. The absence or underdevelopment of political science as a discipline at English-language universities represents another case in point, and cannot solely be explained by the English exclusion from politics and public administration in preference for commerce and industry. While it is to a certain extent understandable that dependant younger scholars, keen to receive a degree, are hesitant to jeopardise a career by becoming involved in disputes with the powers that be, the same considerations do not apply in the case of well-established chairholders, who nevertheless often continue their harmless academic hobby. At some of the black universities, notably Durban-Westville, the pressure of accommodation on the black staff has been so successful that black faculty are often more despised by politicised students than their white, domineering counterparts. Privatism sometimes also takes the form of seemingly radical, though highly general and abstract, writing whose vagueness and concern with theoretical issues renders any relationship to South Africa's social problems dubious. Some observers have charged that in the South African case 'the injunction to be apolitical becomes a precept of amorality' (van den Berghe, 1970, p. 171).

Exile

Exile of South African academics represents a removal from effective impacts on domestic politics, though many exiles initially believe that they can fight for their cause better outside the Republic. However, they soon find themselves cut off from the vital exposure to the local political atmosphere which would seem an essential prerequisite for sober political judgements and can only be partially substituted by reading, correspondence and contact with fellow exiles. Difficulties of adjustment to a new environment, together with guilt feelings for having abandoned the cause at home, sometimes explain odd behaviour. John Marcum (1972, pp. 262-75) has perceptively analysed the revolutionary ineffectiveness caused by this 'exile-syndrome'. With the unexpected indifference of an outside world, at first believed to be receptive to the plight of opponents of apartheid, the quest to become an authentic refugee sometimes leads to imaginative exaggerations. Without the stature of a Solzhenitsyn, some exiles nevertheless denounce any sceptics in the name of special knowledge. While the exiled intellectual for the first time has the advantage of unrestricted access to prohibited sources[2] and multi-faceted viewpoints, much exile writing on South Africa is marred by an unbalanced, emotional perspective, such as, for instance, the conclusion of a recent article in a scholarly journal by a former NUSAS president: 'The truest view of South Africa is not the view from the finance-houses of Johannesburg or the suburbs of Cape Town or the Department of Economics at this or that university, but the view from Makana (the prison) Island' (Driver, 1975, p. 119).

Whether exile was forced upon individuals through intolerable conditions, and must therefore for the time being be considered indefinite, or whether it was chosen voluntarily, with the option to return, would seem to be an important difference. While South Africa always had a net outward brain drain to the centre for opportunistic reasons, there has been an additional substantial migration of politically disenchanted scholars, particularly during the early sixties. British and North American universities, particularly in the politically sensitive disciplines, are full of former South Africans who have made rapid progress in their careers and often distinguished themselves as renowned figures in their field. In some ways, this subtle exodus may be compared with the more publicised flight of the German Jews in the thirties. To my knowledge, no study has yet been attempted to assess the overall impact of this migration on the South African 'open' universities, many of whose present members of faculty would not hold the same positions had the voluntary exiles remained. Given the ill-advised boycott of South African universities by overseas liberal academics, and therefore the greater chances of apolitical applicants from abroad, it is surprising that the open universities have remained as liberal in their self-concept as they have done.

Liberal retreat

The uncompromising insistence on a common non-racialist society in the face of its overwhelming obstacles, seems to constitute the most principled intellectual stance. Liberals have no illusion about their isolation. As Kuper (1974, p. 266) has put it:

There can be little doubt that liberals are not viable in extreme racial conflicts. They have no mass following, they have no skill in, nor inclination for, violence. In consequence they are easily emasculated by governmental repression, or liquidated by extremists on both sides.

And yet liberal South African academics continue to proclaim against all odds the ideal of what Alan Paton (1971, p. 45) has called 'the apocalyptic vision which sees a world where the wolf lies down with the lamb'; they denounce injustices; they affirm faith in constitutional reforms, universal suffrage and an independent judiciary (Mathews, 1971) or publish blueprints of a harmonious 'Federation of Southern Africa' (Marquard, 1971). Above all, liberal intellectuals 'encourage interracial cooperation' and believe in, or hope for, 'continuity in structure and culture' (Kuper, 1974, p. 273), or more concretely, 'that there are no group differences which divide us as much as friendship and our common humanity unite us' (Brookes, 1973, p. 243).

In political terms, the liberal dream amounts to an internal exile. In contrast to their journal *Reality*, liberals do not face South African reality. The insistence on colour-blindness in a society in which all life-chances are determined by colour neither eliminates this fact, nor does it contribute to an adequate awareness of it. Moreover, as an involuntary participant in the privileges, the white liberal lives in guilt and cannot relate naturally across the colour bar, even if it were possible. Whether the white liberal is blind or sensitive to this fact is irrelevant compared with the objective fact of his status, and the perception of that rank by blacks in a colour-conscious environment. Equal status contact is excluded in conditions of vast discrepancies of wealth and power. While the liberal academic lives in the illusion that these factors can be temporarily set aside on a personal level, outside observers have frequently commented on the phoniness of such contacts:

> Recent white converts to nonracialism behave unnaturally under the strain of trying to be 'natural' and remain conscious of their unconventionality — which they display with the self-complacency and titillation of one who has entered a daring, reckless bohemia (van den Berghe, 1970, pp. 164-5).

Politicised black intellectuals have long rejected this inevitable paternalism in the liberal goal of integration into an essentially white society, for which the black has to qualify. Black consciousness (Adam,

1973, pp. 149-65) views South African society in group terms, and it is interesting that progressive white intellectuals have responded with a programme of 'white consciousness' (Nettleton, 1972, p. 8) which conceives of itself as avoiding the liberal schizophrenia without being racist. The difference between this concept and the traditional white colour consciousness lies in the implied dependency and domination in the latter and the envisaged equality of group relations in the former. According to this perspective, critical whites would no longer have to apologise and feel guilty about an accident of birth, and black intellectuals would have shed internalised inferiority feelings.

Why do liberal academics object to this group identification? One could argue that the true modern intellectual, especially in the English tradition, has his value system oriented towards a world culture rather than a local context This intellectual strength — universalism versus particularism — signals at the same time political weakness. Gouldner (1975, p. 20) has recently reiterated this old insight by stating:

> Intellectuals, then, may be at home almost anywhere. Or they may be homeless anywhere, feeling an alienation from all particularistic, history-bound places, and feeling separated from an everyday-life unintelligible except to those sharing the same tacit background assumptions.

While Mannheim's (1936, 1960) free-floating intelligentsia without social interests amounts to a myth, important factors of the intellectual condition, not the least language and a reasoned discourse, set intellectuals apart from everyday perceptions around them. No strong motivation to overcome this division seems easily successful, as the student militants found out when their jargon failed to communicate with the much sought after proletarian masses. Genuine community-rootedness seems almost incompatible with a transcending universal vision which reduces the sensitivity to the surrounding object and target for change. This indeed might constitute the decisive difference between a successful politician and a genuine intellectual.

In the South African situation, moreover, what distinguishes the historical role of white intellectuals from their historical predecessors or contemporary colleagues in Third World societies is the certainty that white intellectuals will not be the actual or spiritual leaders of the historical agent of transformation in South Africa. Unlike the Jacobins, the Young Hegelians and later the Marxists in the Russian Revolution, the blacks in South Africa would no longer tolerate a vanguard from outside their group, be it of the liberal version, NUSAS students, the union organisers of multiracial TUCSA or the non-African communists in the African National Congress. This relegates the white intellectual essentially to the role of spectator and throws him back into his own group for any meaningful praxis. His system of symbols, of which skin colour is not the least important, is different and thereby stifles access to political mobilisation. White intellectuals can feel as much outrage against their own group and genuine identification with the subordinates, and yet, it is the blacks' struggle and not theirs. Even if they have the cleanest credentials, have been banned or suffered imprisonment for their cause, this does not in the end alter the picture. Liberals 'have become isolates' and 'are everywhere in retreat' not only because they are 'subjected to the most articulate vituperation' from every quarter, as Kuper (1974, p. 272) regrets, but partly because they failed to comprehend their own position with their universalistic orientation as *Weltbürger* which does not correspond with a differently structured reality.

The militant-radical stance

The militant-radical stance differs from the liberal opposition in its rejection of reformist measures, its advocacy of confrontation and polarisation and ultimately, if necessary, the use of violence, as suitable tactics to bring about desired changes. South African academics still in the country who would fall into this category are very few, their number is often exaggerated by the authorities and not all those actually prosecuted would identify themselves with these perspectives. Nevertheless, the militant orientation has some actual, and more potential, appeal, particularly for some black students, who out of desperation cannot see any other alternatives for rapid change and meaningful self-assertion. Intellectuals in this category range in their ideological outlook from radical clerics to genuine socialists, from mere moralists to African nationalists. Only in rare instances do they seem to be associated with banned underground organisations, involved in self-proclaimed 'armed struggle'.

Apart from the moral reprehension against the use of violence to achieve a non-violent society, particularly when the exhortations emanate from the safe shelter of academia abroad, there are several neglected pragmatic arguments. (1) As Kuper (1974) has perceptively pointed out, the failure of non-violence in earlier periods does not logically imply that the opposite will succeed. (2) Contrary to Fanon, the oppressed are not always justified in taking up arms, because their violence could make matters worse for everybody, themselves included (Barrington Moore, 1970, p. 28). (3) Violence against things but not people is no answer either, because things are usually protected by people who inevitably become the target. While most critical intellectuals would not denounce violence *per se* and under any circumstances (for instance in clear self-defence or against a personal dictatorship, such as Nazi Germany where the costs and benefits were rationally calculable), South African dissenters almost unanimously agree that the use of violence under the given circumstances is counter-productive and amounts to suicide. Moreover, martyrdom, as Nietzsche has stressed, cannot be a valid argument for a cause.

Nevertheless, there is occasionally the tendency to view persecution as moral demonstration, rather than defeat. In a masochistic fashion, the isolation is glorified; rendering opponents ineffective by ministerial decree does not amount to an easy success of the system in this perspective, but is said to reveal its weakness.[3] In their political ineffectiveness, the militant radicals are as apolitical as the liberals, interested in demonstrative purity, not results: 'What is more, we tend to forget that the lives and examples of those who tried to perform these duties and carry out these obligations are the real treasures of the Church, not their political and social achievements' (Paton, 1971, p. 49).

It would seem that this moralistic, as opposed to a political, perspective also permeates the arguments about the proper role of South African universities, which are said to have a duty to be at least outspoken 'witnesses'. A history of ideas would point to the important difference between this outlook and an interest-based, Marxist-inspired, sociological perspective in which morality is only a political factor of mobilisation. South African dissent, hardly through its own fault, frequently lacks this dimension and, therefore, appears strangely naive abroad. Much of the social science writing in Western Europe and to a lesser extent in North America, even in its most perceptive conservative versions, for example Shils (1972), is admittedly inspired by its exposure to and refutation of socialist/Marxist challenges. If there is a single deficiency in most research and political theories emanating from South Africa, it would seem to lie in that exclusion from a most fundamental debate. The zeal with which the government clamps down on any ideas associated with Marxism not only perpetuates ignorance of an essential component of modern Western thought, but also attributes overrated powers of persuasion to an outdated doctrine. In any case, deprived black workers in South Africa, even if they had the inclination, would hardly have to read Marx in order to become radicalised. Most

intellectuals on the other hand are likely to become thoroughly
immunised against communist sympathies by an unhindered study of its
totalitarian practice and its sophisticated left critics, while at present
the suppressed ideology holds the attraction of the forbidden and,
therefore, the false promise of an alternative for the uninformed. Ralf
Dahrendorf (1969, p. 51) once stressed that 'each position whose
opposite is not discussed is a weak position'. Meanwhile the South
African public is fed with crude notions of the 'communist threat' as a
new version of *die swart gevaar* — which lumps together Fabian
socialists, guilt-ridden clerics, African nationalists, Trotskyites, bureau-
crats with imperial ambitions in Moscow and frightened Maoists, in a
monolithic conspiracy against the South African 'bastion of civilisation'
— at a time when the socialist bloc is breaking up in unseen sectarian
fratricide. Instead of moralising, radical intellectuals could educate a
bewildered South African public for the fast-approaching day when its
government will have to deal with communist-inclusive coalitions in
Italy and France or even a Red Chinese ambassador in Pretoria, as some
Afrikaner academics have recently advocated (sociologist Ben Piek at
Rand Afrikaans University, cited *The Star*, WE, 10 April 1976). There is
little hope of a more progressive reorientation of white attitudes in the
absence of an adequate global perspective, and here the intellectual
opinion-makers again must set the pace.

Change through association

On a scale of dissent, the opposite end of the militant radicals would be
occupied by those intellectuals who have adopted the tactic of working
through association with those in power for a gradual shift and the
amelioration of harsh measures. Their strategic placement within the
system offers protection and at the same time affords real hope for
small improvements in an overall stalemate. Many Afrikaner academics,
and also blacks within the separate development institutions, have
chosen this path of opposition to a greater or lesser degree. The temptation to allow co-optation and transform themselves into mandarins of
power is ever present. If they betray their ideals and fully join the rank
of the rulers in the name of pragmatism and expediency, they may have
become part of the intelligentsia but certainly cease to be intellectuals.
The tangible rewards for co-optation are much greater than for the continuation of the critical role, which, in the extreme case of some
Afrikaners, carries the heavy burden of ostracism by a still relatively
cohesive elite.

Dahrendorf (1969, p. 50) has ascribed to intellectuals the role of medieval fools, the 'court jesters of modern society' who act as the critical conscience of the rulers. However, there is little that is funny in South Africa and the profound function of the fool would depend on the thin tolerance of the ruler. Moreover, in polarised conflicts it is seldom admitted that the true patriot might be the traitor to group solidarity. More appropriate for the Afrikaner academic might be the role of ideological *voortrekker*, venturing into new pastures with the knowledge that the imagined enemy does not exist. His message would aim at breaking the spell of conformist pressures by strengthening the ego of autonomous, self-critical individuals who no longer need the crutches of blind group identification for relief from anxieties. While the emancipatory effort of the Afrikaner intellectuals lies in universalising ethnocentric group identities, the black intellectual faces the opposite task of strengthening ethnic solidarity in order to prevent fragmentation.

Political reformers

From the unknown number of dissenters in association with the ruling power must be distinguished those who openly involve themselves in competing legal organisations. Though they adhere to the rules of the system, they have declared themselves publicly in favour of substantial modification and are prepared to work for it in counter-organisations, be they political parties or other voluntary associations. Their tactics consist of gradual reforms of existing institutions with the goal of increasing liberalisation, rather than the abolition of central core values. Every piecemeal success towards non-racialism is welcomed, rather than ridiculed. A substantial number, though still overall a small minority of South African academics at the English-language universities, joined by a few Afrikaner colleagues, have become involved in this praxis, often the same persons being active in several organisations. They form their own mutually rewarding subculture, in response to official rhetorical attacks and intimidation, but few cases of actual persecution.

The role of reformers in South Africa benefits from a special leverage. Unlike totalitarian systems which can cynically dismiss their internal opponents, apartheid as an ideological blueprint is not merely the implementation of superior power, but justifies this coercion with an elaborate set of theoretical assumptions in its quest for legitimacy. Critical scholars can challenge the scientific articulation of official ideology, they can confront the claims with a contradictory reality and redefine the issues, so that their opponent is on the defensive. For this purpose alone, reformers have to seek dialogue rather than the smug isolation of the ivory tower. Like the 'intellectual guerrillas' who work for change through rational persuasion in association with those in power, the reformers aim at de-traumatising the public by speaking the unspeakable rather than accommodating existing sentiments for short-term political gains. Above all, they clarify and concretise viable alternatives and thereby remove fears which are associated with the so far rather abstract designs.[4]

In addition to this broad area which might be subsumed under the heading 'consciousness-raising and politicisation' there is the vast field of direct involvement with immediate needs in which some university members play an important part. By redefining research priorities some faculties have become involved in the solution of pressing community problems beyond charity, paternalism and tutelage. Examples are the establishment of legal clinics by law faculties, medical care, nutrition and health promotion for the poor rather than the privileged, the planning of decent housing for blacks by departments of architecture, educational assistance in urban training projects, wage commissions and research for trade unions. There is still wide scope for reformist imagination and experimentation despite the rigidities of racial structures.[5]

Of course, there will be those who charge that reforms will merely streamline the existing system and make it less vulnerable. Surely, 'a more comfortable prison is not to be confused with freedom', as Wallerstein (1975, p. 29) argues in ridiculing 'liberalisation' in South Africa. But he forgets to add that it is for the inmates to reject the improvement. If a personal statement may be allowed for concluding: If I were an inmate, I would opt and strive for as many improvements as possible — without abandoning the utopia, which in the end might perhaps be composed of the accumulation of small and much derided piecemeal reforms, 'revolutions at the micro-level' (Galtung, cited Kuper, 1974, p. 102), rather than the often totalitarian and impossible grand design.

Notes

1. This analysis represents essentially the view of an outsider (German by university education, but having taught in Canada for the last ten years), who has never had to face personally the predicaments discussed. However, the author's empathy with the situation of South African colleagues dates back to a visiting appointment at the University of Natal in 1967 and subsequent regular, almost annual, visits to South Africa, motivated by family ties as well as continuing research interests. Two erstwhile South African academics, Kogila Adam-Moodley and Hamish Dickie-Clark, have kindly commented on this essay and their criticisms

were greatly appreciated.

2. Over 26,000 publications are reported to be 'banned' in South Africa (Academic Freedom Committees, 1974), p. 28.

3. Typical of this attitude were comments, reported to have been made by Cosmas Desmond, a former Catholic priest, after his banning order was lifted: 'In any struggle there must be suffering, there must be martyrs. They are a living testimony to the oppressive character of an insecure regime' (*The Star*, WE, 27 September 1975, 15). In his guilt feelings about his predetermined advantage, compared with the black victim, the white radical even bemoans his freedom, as if he has to blame himself for the predicament: 'I was a privileged banned and house-arrested person. Now I am a privileged "free" person and that is even more difficult to live with' (ibid.).

4. In terms of political impact it would seem that one of the crucial short-comings of such central documents as the *Freedom Charter* or the Progressive Party's programme, let alone the United Party, is its abstract and general nature which does not spell out in detail crucial economic and constitutional changes envisaged. Not only can this vagueness be exploited by the political opponent and associated with various anxieties, it also is the cause for disunity rather than the widest common denominator in the reform movement. Nationalist policy, on the future of Africans at least, is much more precise.

5. An important institutional response by South African universities could be to provide not only a niche for the survival of all forms of dissent in the tradition of academic freedom but actively to encourage and reward all political involvement by university faculty rather than only the traditional, problem-neutral scholarship. During the considerations for promotion, tenure and salary increases in many Canadian universities the fourth criterion, besides teaching, traditional research and administrative contribution, is 'community service' in whichever form the individual chooses to engage in it. There are very few activities in South Africa which have no political implications and an encouragement of such involvement by its most skilled section of citizenry could help to break the stalemate of complacency and false normality in the country.

References

Academic Freedom Committees of the University of Cape Town and the University of the Witwatersrand, Johannesburg, *The Open Universities in South Africa and Academic Freedom 1957-1974*, (Juta, Cape Town, 1974)

Adam, Heribert 'The Rise of Black Consciousness in South Africa', *Race* (October 1973), XV, 2, pp.149-65

Beals, Ralph L. *The Politics of Social Research. An Inquiry into the Ethics and Responsibilities of Social Scientists* (Aldine, Chicago, 1969)

Brookes, Edgar H. 'Minority Report', in SPROCAS, *South Africa's Political Alternatives* (Ravan Press, Johannesburg, 1973)

Dahrendorf, Ralf 'The Intellectual and Society: The Social Function of the "Fool" in the Twentieth Century', in Philip Rieff (ed.), *On Intellectuals* (Doubleday, New York, 1969)

Driver, C.J. 'The View from Makara Island, Some Recent Prison Books from South Africa', *Journal of Southern African Studies*, (1975) 2, No.1, pp.109-119.

Fanon, Franz *The Wretched of the Earth* (Grove Press, New York, 1963)

Gouldner, Alvin W. 'Prologue to a Theory of Revolutionary Intellectuals', *Telos* (Winter 1975-76), 26, pp. 3-36

Habermas, Jürgen *Protestbewegung und Hochschulreform* (Suhrkamp, Frankfurt, 1969)

Kuper, Leo *Race, Class and Power. Ideology and Revolutionary Change in Plural*

Societies (Aldine, Chicago, 1974)

Mannheim, Karl *Ideology and Utopia* (Routledge & Kegan Paul, London (1936, 1960)

Marcum, John A. 'The Exile Condition and Revolutionary Effectiveness: Southern African Liberation Movements', in Christian P. Potholm and Richard Dale (eds.), *Southern Africa in Perspective Essays in Regional Politics* (The Free Press, New York, 1972), pp. 262-75

Marquard, Leo *A Federation of Southern Africa* (Oxford University Press, London, 1971)

Mathews, A.S. *Law, Order and Liberty in South Africa* (Juta, Cape Town, 1971)

Moore, Barrington, *Reflections on the Causes of Human Misery and Upon Certain Proposals to Eliminate Them* (Beacon Press, Boston, 1970)

Nettl, J.P. 'Ideas, Intellectuals, and Structures of Dissent', in Philip Rieff (ed.), *On Intellectuals* (Doubleday, New York, 1969), pp. 53-124

Nettleton, Clive 'The White Problem', in SPROCAS, *White Liberation* (Ravan Press, Johannesburg, 1972), pp. 7-24

Paton, Alan 'Some Thoughts on the Common Society', in SPROCAS (Occasional Publication no. 3), *Directions of Change in South African Politics* (Johannesburg, 1971)

Shils, Edward *The Intellectuals and the Powers* (The University of Chicago Press, Chicago, 1972)

SPROCAS, *White Liberation* (Ravan Press, Johannesburg, 1972)

van den Berghe, Pierre *Race and Ethnicity. Essays in Comparative Sociology*, (Basic Books, New York, 1970)

Wallerstein, Immanuel 'Disengagement as a Tactic in the Liberation of Southern Africa', in *Study Project on External Investment in South Africa and Namibia (S.W. Africa), The Policy Debate* (Africa Publication Trust, Uppsala, 1975)

Weber, Max 'Wissenschaft als Beruf', in *Gesammelte Aufsätze zur Wissenschaftslehre* (J.C.B. Mohr, Tübingen, (1919), 1968), pp. 582-613

Welsh, David 'Social Research in a Divided Society: The Case of South Africa', *Social Dynamics* (1975), 1, pp. 19-30

3 COMMITMENT: THE LIBERAL AS SCHOLAR IN SOUTH AFRICA

Hilda Kuper

To reflect on the position of the liberal as scholar in South Africa is to consider a particular case of a more general phenomenon — the place of the intellectual as humanist in a hostile and repressive milieu. I restrict myself in this essay to three specific questions posed in terms of the historical conditions of South Africa as a plural society.[1] In this context in which a white minority monopolises power and manipulates the concept of race for the maintenance of its privileges, what is the content and thrust of liberalism? Why is 'liberalism' frequently misrepresented and the term 'liberal' used as an epithet of abuse and why do the extreme right, represented by the South African government, and the radical left join forces in the attack on liberalism? What choices are open to the liberal intellectual in South Africa, and is it possible for him to be ethically neutral in a society so weighted with social discrimination and oppression?

I

Liberalism as a humanist philosophy has a history that can be traced back to the Judaic-Christian-Greek intellectual world along with ideas of liberty and liberalism with which it is closely linked.[2] It need not be, indeed it seldom is, confined to a single political party, nor limited to any economic programme, nor tied to the social power of any one class. It has the spirit of freedom as its credo, and as such it is not restricted to time and place.

While the essence of liberalism is an awareness of the value of freedom and of the human worth of the individual, its policy direction depends on lines of existing oppression and exclusion in a particular society at a particular period of time. In the context of the Enlightenment it referred to freedom of inquiry, freedom of the spirit, freedom to seek for truth. In England it first took the form of demands for religious liberty and tolerance, constitutionalism and political rights. In South Africa the emphasis has been on non-racism, on freedom from racial discrimination, and on the protection of individual liberty.

The initial line of action, modelled by liberals in the Cape on policy transplanted from Britain, was directed to an extension of the franchise by criteria of 'civilisation' and to securing of civil rights. Despite the ethnocentric interpretation of 'civilisation' in terms of western criteria of education and wealth, the acceptance of a shared humanity was unquestioned. The nineteenth century British approach to liberalism expressed in the Cape was submerged at the time of Union when, in the struggle between Boer and British, the more narrow nationalism of the Boer Republics prevailed and the basis of the present policy was laid in 1910, in the Act of Union. In 1939, Professor Hoernlé wrote: 'In short, subject to the over-arching fact of White domination, the South African native policy is an odd patchwork exhibiting traces of Parallelism, Assimilation, Separation' (p. 159). The Afrikaner Nationalist Party (NP) which first came into power in 1948 established its fortification on ground already prepared. However, it extended and entrenched domination through a consistent political system in which laws governing race relations and dehumanising individual relations were deliberately pla planned within the totalitarian ideology of apartheid.

The passage of these laws and their implementation established apartheid in the law-abiding sentiments of the electorate, involved more and more people in the administration of apartheid 'converting its basic concepts into the routine of office' (Kuper, 1956, p. 209). There was a terrifying, almost lunatic 'rationality' as laws moved from the prohibition of body contact to prohibition of the exchange of ideas: The Prohibition of Mixed Marriages Act of 1949; the Immorality Amendment Act of 1950; the Group Areas Act of 1950; the Bantu Education Act of 1953. The overall administrative framework sealing off each individual life in a government-specified racial cage was provided by the Population Registration Act no. 30 of 1950; the basic artillery preventing escape to freedom was the Suppression of Communism Act, no. 44 of 1950, which extended the definition of communism to what has been described as 'statutory communism.'[3]

But the process of domination and of dehumanisation is far from complete, not because of weakness on the part of the government, but because of the resilience of ideas of liberalism and of human dignity in the oppressed. Concepts of individual worth, self-respect, and a general humanity are not unique to 'enlightened' western societies! There is a strange arrogance in equating liberalism with whites, when it is a humanist philosophy to which many peoples of different races have contributed in the long history of continuously renewed struggles for freedom. In my own experience, some of the finest liberals I have met were among the leaders of the African National Congress (ANC). Chief Luthuli, formerly president of the ANC, was the very embodiment of liberal ideals.

Among the Bantu-speaking peoples of southern Africa the notion of humanism is expressed as an abstract noun derived from the archaic root for 'person'. A rich body of anthropological writings reveals the control on despotism, and national and individual ideals of freedom and dignity in a range of traditional African states.[4] I am not here concerned with the details of these systems; more significant is the fact that such African leaders of the African National Congress as P. Ka I. Seme, Dr A.B. Xuma, Chief Albert Luthuli, perceived the liberal democratic elements in and drew inspiration from their African heritage.[5] They stressed the hierarchy of courts that protected individuals from arbitrary injustice; the opportunity for an accused to state his case and express his opinions; the participation of all adults in the deliberations of councils of the nation; the effort to reach consensus by discussion; the economic security that followed from the fact that the land belonged to the people and that every man and woman had the right to a site for his home and for fields to grow food; and the morality and respect for the individual present in a pervasive religious system. They acknowledged that tensions were present — as in all social life — but the sense of freedom and human worth was deeply rooted. Bad leaders ran the risk of losing their followers, and tyrants that of assassination. Mission-educated Africans were often taught to downgrade their own cultures, but there were also missionaries who expressed admiration for the deeply religious outlook that permeated African life. Increasingly Africans found that the fundamental ethics of the Judaic-Christian tradition were not incompatible with those of their own forefathers.

Until 1961 the only methods of political action used and accepted by the African National Congress were non-violent and their goals were justice and equality for all. The outlook was that of a liberal humanism. It was this spirit that gave substance to the Non-Violent Resistance Campaign of 1952 in which more than 8,500 volunteers, mainly African, courted arrest and imprisonment by committing acts of civil disobedience in protest against the Pass laws, the Group Areas Act, the Separate Representation of Voters Act and the Stock Limitation Acts for the African Reserves — laws symbolising white domination and privilege. Tragic rioting at various centres, triggered off by superficially minor incidents, gave the government the opportunity to introduce further repressive legislation and frighteningly severe penalties. Two new categories of offence were created: inviting anyone to protest against any law and accepting any assistance, financial or other, for organised protest. The penalties were heavy, a fine of £1,000, imprisonment for five years, ten lashes or a combination of any of these; for a second or subsequent conviction, whipping or imprisonment were mandatory.

The Liberal Party came into existence in the aftermath of the Campaign. The Afrikaner Nationalist Party (NP) had gained its second victory. The United Party (UP), the official opposition, supported mainly by English-speaking whites, was equally committed to a policy of white domination. There were at that time three representatives elected by Africans in the Lower House, and four representatives in the Senate, a deviation from apartheid which the NP was pledged to eradicate. Four of these Representatives, rejecting any alliance with the UP, became the first and only members of the Liberal Party (LP) in Parliament. The party was committed not only to the general principle of a common society, but specifically to the abolition of all colour bars and to a citizenship open to all races (Ballinger, 1969, p. 402). An initial policy of a qualified franchise was soon challenged by its own white as well as African and Indian members, and its policy steadily moved close to that of a welfare state. Its program specified the removal of all discriminatory legislation, the protection of individual rights, a universal franchise on a common voters' roll, an equitable redistribution of land, nationalisation of essential services, free and compulsory education for all, and an ultimate objective of social security for all its peoples. The energies of most liberals, however, were directed not to parliamentary debate but to the pursuit of liberal policies in everyday life. The number of Africans in the Liberal Party was increasing through active positive cooperation against racial injustice in rural areas as well as in the towns. Among the most effective and dedicated LP workers were Peter Brown and his fellow worker, Elliott Mngadi; they were to be amongst the many victimised by the Nationalist government — arrested, and banned for a long period.

Relations with the African National Congress were initially good, based on mutual trust as well as personal friendships. While it may be true that certain whites who called themselves liberals had a paternalist attitude to 'others', this was patently not true for the majority. There is something ludicrous in the fact that this charge comes so often from communists, who are convinced that communism is the correct doctrine, which must be imposed on the people in their own interest, an attitude quite reminiscent of early rigid missionary zeal. Liberalism, by contrast, is essentially more flexible, more egalitarian, more conscious of the value of liberty and the dignity of all, and cooperative in the search for effective policies.

Official relations between the Liberal Party and the ANC deteriorated for a while when the LP declined an invitation to be a partner in the planning of the 'Congress of the People'. This decision was taken on the initiative of the Transvaal branch of the Liberal Party, to whom negotiations had been delegated, on the grounds that the plans had already been completed, and that the offer to cooperate was not a genuine offer. This was a decision regretted by many liberals. The Freedom Charter which was endorsed by the Congress of the People was a fine document, expressing basic democratic principles. No doubt for this reason, on 5 December 1956, 156 men and women, associated with the Congress of the People, were arrested and charged, under the Suppression of Communism Act, with a treasonable conspiracy inspired by international communism to overthrow the South African State by violence. The trial dragged on for four and a half years. The offence of treason is punishable by death. But those who were released, and others who had not been charged, carried on.

This was a period of continued cooperation between the Liberal Party and the Congresses. In October 1958, Chief Luthuli, President of the ANC, released after many months of tension, stated:

> I welcome the presence of the Liberal Party. It stands for and represents lasting values, values which would make South Africa a country to be honoured. We in the A.N.C. would particularly like to work with the Liberal Party. I must say that we do usually cooperate in those matters where we agree and as the years have gone by we have found ourselves more and more in agreement with the Liberal Party. (*Contact*, 1 Nov. 1958, quoted in Robertson, 1971, p. 183)

Nineteen hundred and sixty (1960) was to be Africa Year; in South Africa it was to be anti-pass year. The more militant and exclusive Pan-African Congress (PAC) which had split from the ANC called for mass protests. The police opened fire on unarmed African demonstrators; at Sharpeville 69 were killed and 180 wounded; at Langa two were killed and 49 wounded. The ANC called for a strike as a national day of mourning. This killing evoked such criticism that it was rumoured that the Government would suspend the pass laws. Chief Luthuli publicly burnt his pass, followed by thousands of others. But the government declared a state of emergency, and banned the ANC and the PAC; it did not matter that after the longest and fullest trial the judge found those accused of treason not guilty.

Under persistent oppression, and rejection by the government of all democratic techniques ranging from petitions to boycotts, former adherents of peace turned to acts of sabotage. They formed the Spear of the Nation (*Umkhonto we Sizwe*). This was an organisation outside the African National Congress: and though Congress leaders had worked closely with the Communist Party, the ANC still did not accept communism as its creed. At the 'Rivonia Trial', in which the accused were charged with sabotage and treasonable conspiracy, Nelson Mandela, the first accused and President of the banned ANC, gave with controlled passion the reasons for his planning of *Umkhonto we Sizwe* — 'not in a spirit of recklessness, nor because of any love of violence but as a result of a calm and sober assessment of the political situation that had arisen after many years of tyranny, exploitation and oppression of my people by the whites' (Mandela, 1965, p. 163). In the course of his lengthy statement in which he expressed his appreciation of the open and constant support of dedicated communists in South Africa he also said:

> As far as the Communist Party is concerned, and if I understand its policy correctly, it stands for the establishment of a State based on the principles of Marxism. Although it is prepared to work for the Freedom Charter, as a short-term solution to the problems created by White supremacy, it regards the Freedom Charter as the beginning, and not the end, of its programme.
>
> The ANC, unlike the Communist Party, admitted Africans only as members. Its chief goal was, and is, for the African people to win unity and full political rights. The Communist Party's main aim, on the other hand, was to remove the capitalists and to replace them with a working-class government. The Communist Party sought to emphasize class distinctions whilst the ANC seeks to harmonize them. This is a vital distinction.
>
> It is true that there has often been close cooperation between the ANC and the Communist Party. But cooperation is merely proof of a common goal — in this case the removal of white supremacy — and is not proof of a complete community of interests. (ibid, p. 179.)

A few members of the Liberal Party also turned to violence, establishing the African Resistance Movement outside of the Liberal Party. Spokesmen for the Party stressed that the primary cause of sabotage in South Africa was the policy of apartheid, though as a party it judged saboteurs harshly. In fact, the relationship between liberalism and violence has varied from country to country; in Great

Britain liberalism was established by a gradual process of reform; in France the call to liberty, equality and fraternity was accompanied by bloodshed and bitterness as well as sweeping reconstructions. In South Africa, the Liberal Party was committed to non-violence.[6]

The Liberal Party dissolved itself in 1968 when 'The Prohibition of Improper Interference Act' made interracial political activity illegal and membership of any interracial organisation a criminal offence. Since then, the meeting ground for whites and blacks has been narrowed and the possibility of non-violent change has become less likely. In the process of polarisation, the liberal — irrespective of colour — becomes the target of extremists on both sides. The most recent victims of government repression include members of the Institute of Race Relations, the Christian Institute, NUSAS (National Union of Students), and militant liberals in all walks of life. The social basis of liberalism in South Africa is not an intellectual elite, but people of all classes and all races, in which Africans and Indians constitute the great majority.

II

The particular expression of any general political philosophy is related to conditions of time and place; in South Africa, with its extreme racial oppression, the preoccupation of liberals, as I indicated above, has been with the removal of racial discrimination. To apply to South Africa a 'liberal position' described for very different societies and in quite different periods produces a gross distortion of that position.

Martin Lipset, in a discussion of liberalism, presents the following model:

> in economics — a commitment to laissez-faire ideology, a belief in the vitality of small business, and opposition to strong trade-unions; in politics — a demand for minimal government intervention and regulation; in social ideology — support of equal opportunity for achievement, opposition to aristocracy, and opposition to enforced equality of income; in culture — anticlericalism and antitraditionalism (p. 129).

But he begins this description by locating his analysis:

> In Europe where it (liberalism) is represented by various parties like the French Radicals, the Dutch and Belgian liberals, the liberal position means ... (p. 129).

The Liberal as Scholar in South Africa

The policies and goals of the parties in the above-named countries at a particular period are quite foreign to South African liberalism as I have known it in some forty years of involvement and could not be read into the policy of the South African Liberal Party during its short existence. At no stage did it advocate *laissez-faire* capitalism or oppose trade unions. Quite the contrary, its policies tended toward the welfare state.

The ahistoricism so marked in many comments on South African liberalism may be due to ignorance, or careless scholarship, or malice. It is however a widely used technique of misrepresentation. Kovaly describes this mode of distortion in a footnote to *Rehumanization or Dehumanization?* This methodology

> first of all, reduces the philosophic work of a philosopher or social thinker to certain concepts or conceptions that he used, especially to those that were later misused by emptying them of their original content and putting another content into the same concept or conception. Through oversimplification, it is then maintained that these concepts or conceptions are either related, similar or the same. To put it in a different way, one content of the same concept has been substituted for another content, and this methodological stance consists in explaining the concepts as the same or as closely related.
>
> The second step of this methodological operation is to trace one concept or conception in the history of thought from one age to another, disregarding both different social, cultural, scientific or philosophical circumstances and the changes of the content of the particular concept or conception. (1973, p. 144)

There is in fact a complex methodology, a technology of misrepresentation, of South African liberalism. It proceeds very appreciably by direct misrepresentation, by the wrongful attribution of ideas. It might well rest there. But scholars like to proceed in a scholarly way, with integrity and scholarly documentation and proof. And there is now a highly developed technology of scholarly misrepresentation.

The starting point is the *a priori* irrefutable conclusion, which is to be proven. Given this firm starting point, it is child's play to find some statement in a large corpus of writing which may seem to be available as evidence. The basic technique is that of context manipulation. There is the selection, in a most arbitrary fashion, of a writer or writers who are taken to be exemplars of South African liberal thought. Then a sentence, even a phrase, is totally torn from its context and placed in an entirely different context, with deceptive commentary. This is usually sufficient for most purposes. However, sometimes what is to be proven is so remote from, and indeed contrary to, the thinking of the victim, and the critic so lacking in verbal manipulative skill, that he feels obliged to fabricate a quotation by combining phrases from different sections of a book, even going so far as to provide his own linking phrase. But this is unusual, since somewhat the same effect may be achieved by bringing together sentences from different parts of the writing, without hiding the fact, and so combining statements as to give a misleading impression. Occasionally the quotations are reordered, a later quotation preceding an earlier. In the literature of misrepresentation, this is usually a sign that there is dirty work at the crossroads.

The technique of context manipulation may be enhanced by the use of italics. Superficially, it appears that the author is being rather honest and scholarly when he writes 'my italics'. But in the polemical literature of misrepresentation this is far from the case. The critic is using two devices to enhance the misrepresentation. He is adding his own emphasis, and so further removing the quotation from the context in which the author placed it; and the italics are in a way a method of removing the italicised phrase from its context in the quoted sentence. There is a double removal from context.

A more complicated structure of misrepresentation is provided by the mosaic technique. This consists in piecing together a whole series of quotations. I have sometimes been astonished to see a quotation dredged up from a writer's most insignificant work. This does not imply that the critic is saturated in the author's works. On the contrary, there is often a sort of coterie manufacture of misrepresentations. Critic A advances his distortion on the basis of a casual glance at an article, and the manipulation of a sentence or two. Critic B adopts this and adds his own. In a short time there is a seemingly impressive body of documentation, quite unrelated to the works under review. There are two forms of this mosaic technique — one when the structure is pieced together from a single author's writing, and the other when it is fashioned from a whole world of writers.

A most startling example of the second type of mosaic is provided in the long review article by Anthony Atmore and Nancy Westlake titled 'A Liberal Dilemma: A Critique of the Oxford History of South Africa', (*Race*, 2 October 1972, XIV, pp. 107-36). In it, they develop a mosaic of quotations of slightly more than two pages, contained in the writings of six contributors, and culled from a volume of over 500 pages. These quotations are numbered 1-9, giving an impression of scientific precision. All the devices to which I have referred are present. There are the italics in each quotation, there are the dots to show a hiatus, also an important technique of manipulation, and there is the transposition of quotations, a quotation from p. 470 preceding one from p. 466. But above all there is the basic manipulation, quotations torn from their own context, and inserted in the context provided by the critic. It is apparent that, in the use of this method, the possibilities of imputation, of combination, of permutation are infinite.

What is even more startling however is the *a priori* conclusion from which Atmore and Westlake start an early section of their paper. They write that one of the main presuppositions of current liberal ideology, certainly in the South African context, is that modern capitalism is basically an economic and social system which results in the peaceful interaction of, mutual cooperation between, and equivalent benefit to all its participants; that it is 'rational' and 'race blind' (1972, p. 108). The statement is of course totally false. It is difficult to credit that the authors actually believe this. There is a well-known refutation of these views by Herbert Blumer, and the wording of the views ascribed to liberals suggests that the authors had this refutation in mind. In any event, it would be an unusual liberal who subscribed to that point of view.

Many of the contributors to the *Oxford History* were members of the South African Liberal Party, or very close to it in outlook. The programme of the Party was published long before the appearance of the *Oxford History*. It provided for redistribution of land, equal rights, equality of wages and minimum wage levels, nationalisation of essential services, and state intervention in the case of industrial malfunctioning. Yet the methodology of misrepresentation is so effective that the appearance of plausibility and relevance can be given to the superficial reader. And so a false conclusion is demonstrated by the most dubious means. Indeed using the same technique as the critics, and confining oneself to the Atmore and Westlake review article, it should be possible to prove that the authors were practitioners of the Kaballah in seventeenth century Prague. An anagram of their names might be an additional item of proof.

I think the passionate ideological denunciation is greatly to be preferred to many of the academic articles in the literature of misrepresentation, in which one is confronted with the measured language of the scholar and the paraphernalia of scholarship. One knows that these academic articles will be part of a curriculum vitae, items in the bid for promotion, a basis for applications for foundation grants. But one does not know the motivation — an embattled commitment or occupational mobility. It is the masquerade of scholarship which is so distressing, when closer examination reveals much academic legerdemain and scholastic mystification.[7]

Other techniques include the standard propaganda techniques. Thus the word liberal is applied to actions regarded as discreditable, in such a way as to discredit liberals and liberalism. It is for example used in this manner in *Class and Colour in South Africa*, a classic Marxist interpretation based on many years of scholarly research by H.J. and R.E. Simons, who, as members of the Communist Party of South Africa, devoted most of their lives with the greatest courage, integrity and selflessness to the cause of racial and social equality.[8] To them 'liberal' serves as a derogatory term, and so they write on page 322 that the 'liberal professor Edgar Brookes' gave academic backing to the Nationalist Party demand for segregation of Africans. The reference is to the election of 1924. At that time, Edgar Brookes was sympathetic to the Nationalist Party position. It was only years later, as the Simons know perfectly well, that Edgar Brookes became identified with liberalism, a commitment he now maintains with great courage. The views he expressed in support of segregation were not the views of liberals. To take another example, the Simons give an account of the career of Clements Kadalie, the very tough leader of the Industrial and Commercial Union in the 1920s. They offer a number of explanations for his breach with the Communist Party — his criticism of its policies and administration, and the climate of hostility in the country toward communism. But it would seem also that the novelist Ethelreda Lewis was a sort of *femme fatale*, seducing him into political aberration. Indeed there seems to have been a whole seraglio of ideological Delilahs. In a passage on page 368 where the Simons attribute a reactionary point of view to Ethelreda Lewis on minimum wages for Africans, she is described as Kadalie's 'liberal adviser'. Yet when they introduce H. Selby Msimang (p. 225), commenting on his campaign in 1959 to organise African workers in Bloemfontein for an increase in wages, his demand for a minimum wage, and his subsequent arrest and trial on a charge of incitement under the Riotous Assemblies Act, they do not write 'the liberal H. Selby Msimang', even though he was one of the African leaders of the Liberal Party, and remains closely associated with liberalism.

This suggests one further point, the extent to which the multiracial character of liberalism in South Africa is suppressed. The epithet 'white liberal' is very common in the literature of misrepresentation. There was a time in South Africa when the epithet Jewish was often attached to communists, infusing the reaction to communists with anti-Semitism. And so too the epithet 'white liberal' capitalises on racist sentiment in the disparagement of liberalism.

By all these means there has been created a mythology of South African liberalism which seems to be in process of displacing the reality. The political right has its own myths about liberalism. For the proponents of apartheid it represents the very antithesis of their beliefs, the moral challenge to their deeply held values. For the revolutionary left, there is, in part, the traditional conflict between communists and social democrats. But there is a further element. The plain fact that Africans did not respond in large numbers to the stirring slogans of international communism indicated that they had other aspirations for freedom. Liberalism had a great appeal for them, and it thus became a dangerous heresy to be exorcised.

III

The position of the South African liberal scholar is one of commitment. It is a commitment charged with moral indignation at the horrors of apartheid, the terrible suffering it inflicts, its dehumanising content. It is a passionate commitment which does not easily lend itself to the neutral language of the social sciences. And it calls for active involvement in protest and political action. I would agree with C. Wright Mills' comment (1959, p. 29) that 'the most admirable scholars do not split their works from their lives. They seem to take both too seriously to allow such disassociation and they want to use each for the enrichment of the other.'

In *Modernizing Racial Domination* (1971, p. x) Heribert Adam writes as follows:

> From the vast political literature on southern Africa this study differs in perhaps two respects: (1) by its focus on the political economy and the specific dynamics of the South African scene, and (2) in that it tries to avoid the tone of moral indignation frequently present in writings on South Africa. To be sure, there can be no neutrality on the question of racial discrimination, and the argument that it could be worse is indeed a poor rationalization. On the other hand, emotional abhorrence, derived from deep commitment to universal ethics, seems understandable but is no substitute for realistic analysis. The dedicated activist too frequently suffers from illusions arising from wishful thinking.

There seems to be an implication here that the author is initiating realistic political analysis of South African society, which would be a claim hardly grounded in fact. There seems to be a further implication that the expression of moral indignation is not compatible with realistic analysis. But I can see no logical basis for any such assumption. And suppose the writer does feel moral indignation at the racial oppression in apartheid. Will not his whole approach be informed by that indignation? Is objectivity advanced in any way by not expressing that indignation? And indeed, would it not be more consistent with the integrity of scholarship, and with personal integrity, to declare, with anger and commitment, one's revulsion for apartheid.

The social sciences were not created in a void. They developed in response to real problems of human interaction, and in attempts to understand and interpret events experienced by human beings as human beings. The social scientists are themselves part of this reality. The relationship between normative judgement and empirically based knowledge is a fundamental problem for each scholar. Facts do not speak for themselves. They are selected, organised and analysed, within limits culturally as well as personally perceived. The aim of social scientists is to understand the relationships and significance of events and the causes of their being so, for since events (which are imprinted by culture) receive their meaning in the relationship of individuals, their interpretation is always value laden, particularly so in societies characterised by sharp conflict.

Neutral language and a perfunctory commitment to universal values are not be equated with objectivity. The apparent objectivity of a study may be quite spurious, events rapidly undermining its credibility, so that one is left with neither objective realism nor moral commitment. Rationalisation is not explanation, and methodologies are often disguised value judgements. The techniques and vocabulary of social science may readily lend an appearance of dispassionate objectivity, of scientific neutrality. But this may be an 'unethical neutrality', which serves to explain away, not 'explain', oppression in any form and on any scale, so that increasing oppression becomes 'a process of social change', and the more sophisticated techniques are subsumed under 'modernisation'. There are already many serious restraints on freedom of expression in South Africa without accepting further restraints for the sake of an illusory objectivity.

The relationship of knowledge to action is not automatic, nor is one a substitute for the other. Knowledge provides an instrument; action requires decision. The making of a decision is an expression of individual will and accountability, an acceptance of individual responsibility. Writing and teaching, the scholar's most effective modes of action, involve the responsibility of interpreting issues which are politically sensitive. The 'facts' are among the available instruments of power; the dangers of abuse are not always obvious.

For the South African liberal scholar it is hard to express a commitment to scholarship and to liberalism. Based on an assumption of universal values, a critical analysis of the apartheid system inevitably results in an attack on the fundamental structure of that system. Those in power are armed to protect it. Their range of weaponry is wide; state appointed censors are free to ban any publications. Among the banned books recognised outside of South Africa for their admirable scholarship and insights are Kuper's *Passive Resistance in South Africa* and *An African Bourgeoisie*. The first was banned when we were living in South Africa and teaching at the University of Natal; the second, which received the Herskovits Award in 1966, was finished after we had emigrated to America. To possess banned literature or to quote from speeches or writings of a person who is banned, or from a book which is banned, is a criminal offence. At the same time the government runs an extensive 'information service'; its propaganda publications are lavish, persuasive and often 'dispassionate'.

Under the Suppression of Communism Act No. 44 of 1950, persons may be proscribed and organisations liquidated at the arbitrary discretion of the Minister of Justice. Save with his consent or in court proceedings, it is made a criminal offence to record, reproduce, publish or disseminate any speech, utterance, writing or statement, or extract from any of the above, by persons proscribed or liquidated (Sec. 11g). This 'very terrible law is designed to expunge people from the tablets of the living. Indeed, it goes far beyond this. It is an attempt to banish them to external oblivion as if they had never existed' (Kuper, 1974, p. 291). Scholars are obliged by the law to be instruments of this annihilation. Yet some South African scholars, still living in South Africa, write with seeming indifference to the censorship laws. Others seek to convey their meaning, as precisely and accurately as possible, within the constraints of these laws (ibid., p. 310).

Compliance with the censorship laws as a self-protective device is all too understandable; it needs however to be made explicit so that the outside reader is aware of the reality of the repression, its challenge to scholarship, and its threat to the lives of scholars. But I think it goes beyond the permissible limits for a publisher or for a scholar to impose this censorship.[9]

The problem for the scholar is to maintain his individuality and independence, not to lose himself by submission to outside pressure, whether from state or party. Independence, or autonomy, is not a fixed position; it involves a continuous effort in a process of search. An initial event over which the individual has no control, no say, stamps every human being with a crucial identity. This is the paradox of the human condition. An unselected origin in space and time, country, age, parentage, religion, are basic features given at birth. No one is born free. But not all accept apartheid or other forms of oppression. How does one react and why? How interpret the wandering and the quest for freedom of the self and others?

With an unsolicited assortment of physical and cultural attributes, all mixed and fused together, each individual tries to find his own way. For some, it is flat, straight and narrow. For others, full of pitfalls and blind corners. It is seldom smooth and easy. Those with independent spirit run the risk of suffering the fate of Sisyphus, condemned by the gods ceaselessly to roll a rock to the summit of the mountain from which it crashes back inexorably by its own weight. And the struggle of Sisyphus begins again. In the moving interpretation by Camus;

> At each of those moments when he leaves the heights and gradually sinks towards the lairs of the gods, he is superior to his fate. He is stronger than his rock. If this myth is tragic, that is because its hero is conscious. Where would his torture be, indeed, if at every step the hope of succeeding upheld him? . . . The lucidity that was to constitute his torture at the same time crowns his victory. There is no fate that cannot be surmounted by scorn (Camus, 1955, p. 121).

Sisyphus is a symbol; not a type. For Camus, he is the hero in an absurd world, a hero who does not seek escape nor accept illusion, who has the courage to accept a life 'without appeal'. Sisyphus is symbolic of the liberal's continuing struggle in South Africa.

Leo Kuper refers to Camus with admiration and understanding. Camus with his roots in Algiers, his education in France, his sympathy with suffering, his deeply moving accounts of the misery of the Kabyle, long before Algeria became a problem of international concern, his courage in pleading in Algiers, surrounded by hostile settlers, for a truce on the killing of civilians, his anguish at the devastation of violence. Not Sartre who wrote with the passion of hate that in the spilling of blood the oppressed are purified.[10] The passion of Camus (who was not a professional intellectual) is distilled by anguish, an anguish that Leo Kuper reveals in his most recent work *The Pity of It All*. This study of recent events in Algeria, Zanzibar, Rwanda, Burundi describes the escalation of violence until there is no possibility of compromise. The middle ground of mediation is eliminated; extremes are locked in deadly combat; massacre is indiscriminate; the point of no return is reached. Later, perhaps, new structures may be built; but what of the present? Can massacre and carnage be avoided in South Africa? Can the liberal scholar really describe what is happening without emotion?

The Nationalist government remains intransigent. Its much vaunted 'concessions' do not reach the deeper institutionalised structures of inequality. A wedge is being driven into the ranks of liberals; since 'liberalism' is not a pigment, white liberals in South Africa are not visibly distinguishable from other whites. Many have left the country, deserting the field of battle. But many more remain. Black liberals are increasingly isolated. Decolonisation of Angola and Mozambique and the imminent collapse of white minority rule in Rhodesia have opened new possibilities for militant action. Recently school children in the South African township of Soweto rose in protest against their exclusion from the wider world of knowledge, an exclusion built into the degrading system of 'Bantu education', described by the late Luthuli as an attempt at 'brainwashing on a grand scale'. But, he continued 'It will not succeed' (1962, p. 52).

In a situation of mounting crisis the ideal liberal scholar does not retreat into the inviolate sanctuary of academia nor follow the now popular road of those who argue the need for further destruction (an argument too often heard from those outside the danger zone). His is the more difficult, the more lonely task, the search for ways to contain the violence that has been unleashed, a search guided by a lucid mind and a deep humanism, inspired by the example of men and women who in a brutal world have not been brutalised nor terrorised into silence.

Notes

I am grateful for the support I received from the Center for Advanced Study in the Behavioral Sciences and from the National Endowment of the Humanities as a Fellow of the Center 1976-7, on leave from the University of California, Los Angeles.

1. Following Kuper and Smith (1969) I define a plural society as one characterised by structural cleavage, an unequal incorporation in a single state of groups discriminated by race, ethnicity, or religion.
2. Hobhouse (1911); Schapiro (1958).

3. Statutory communism is any doctrine or scheme 'which aims at bringing about any political, industrial, social or economic change within the Union by the promotion of disturbance or disorder, by unlawful acts or omissions or by the threat of such acts or omissions or by means which include the promotion of disturbances or disorder, or such acts or omissions or threats.' For the first illuminating analysis of the rationale and dehumanisation behind the various laws see L. Kuper (1956, pp. 48-72).

4. Gluckman, (1965); Hunter (1936).

5. See, for example. P. Ka I. Seme's articles in his paper, *Abantu Batho*, Luthuli (1962). While Luthuli wrote that Christianity brought to the country a new way of life, a new outlook, a new set of beliefs (p. 20), he also showed the democratic elements in tribal society and in many personal discussions expressed the views I have attributed to him.

6. For a fuller account of how some members of ARM reconciled violence and liberalism, see Robertson (1971, pp. 224-5). She also quotes the official viewpoint expressed by Alan Paton as Chairman at the National Congress in Johannesburg, October 1964.

7. The technique of context manipulation is very similar to the technique of magicians practising illusionary magic, who distract and mystify the public by the presentation of wrong cues. You are so distracted by the wrong cue, that you do not see what they are up to.

8. For a full review of this book see Kuper (1974, pp. 277-87).

9. For a full discussion of this problem, see the account given by L. Kuper of the exclusion of his chapter on African Nationalism in the South African edition of the *Oxford History of South Africa*.

10. Introduction to *The Wretched of the Earth* (Fanon, 1965).

References

Adam, Heribert *Modernizing Racial Domination* (University of California Press, Berkeley, 1971)

Atmore, Anthony and Westlake, Nancy 'A Liberal Dilemma: A Critique of the Oxford History of South Africa', *Race*, (1972), XIV, 2, pp. 107-36

Ballinger, Margaret *From Union to Apartheid* (Praeger, New York, 1969)

Blumer, Herbert 'Industrialization and Race Relations' in Guy Hunter (ed.) *Industrialization and Race Relations* (Oxford University Press, London, 1965)

Camus, Albert *The Myth of Sisyphus and Other Essays* (Alfred Knopf, New York, 1955)

Fanon, Franz *The Wretched of the Earth* (Grove Press, London, 1965)

Gluckman, Max *Politics, Law and Ritual in Tribal Society* (Blackwell, London, 1965)

Hampden-Turner, C.M. 'Radical Man and the Hidden Moralities of Social Science', *Interpersonal Development*, vol. 2, no. 4 (1971-2) pp. 222-37

Hobhouse, L.T. *Liberalism* (Oxford University Press, 1911)

Hoernle, R.F.A. *South African Native Policy and the Liberal Spirit* (University of Cape Town, Cape Town, 1939)

Hunter, Monica *Reaction to Conquest* (Oxford University Press, London, 1936)

Kovaly, Pavel *Rehumanization or Dehumanization?* (Branden Press, Boston, 1973)

Kuper, Leo *Passive Resistance in South Africa* (Jonathan Cape, London, 1956)

——, *An African Bourgeoisie* (Yale University Press, New Haven, 1965)

——, *Race, Class and Power* (Duckworth, London, 1974)

———, *The Pity of It All* (Duckworth, London, 1977)
———, and Smith, M.G. (eds.) *Pluralism in South Africa* (University of California Press, Berkeley, 1969)
Lerner, Max *The Essential Works of John Stuart Mill* (Bantam, New York, 1961)
Lewsen, P. 'The Cape Liberal Tradition – Might or Reality', *Race* (1971) XIII p. 67.
Lipset, S.M. *Political Man* (Doubleday, Garden City NY, 1963)
Luthuli, Albert *Let My People Go* (McGraw Hill, New York, 1962)
Mandela, Nelson *No Easy Walk to Freedom* (Heinemann, 1965)
Riesman, David *Individualism Reconsidered* (Free Press, Macmillan, 1964)
Robertson, Janet *Liberalism in South Africa, 1948-1963* (Clarendon Press, 1971)
Schapiro, J.S. *Liberalism: Its Meaning and History* (Van Nostrand Reinhold Co., New York, 1958)
van den Berghe, P. *South Africa, A Study in Conflict* (Western University Press, 1965)
Walzer, Michael *Obligations* (Harvard University Press, 1970)
Weber, Max 'The Meaning of "Ethical Neutrality" ' in Edward A. Shils and Henry A. Finch (eds.), *The Methodology of the Social Sciences* (The Free Press, Glencoe, Illinois, 1949)
Wright Mills, C. 'On Intellectual Craftsmanship' in *Sociological Theory* (ed.) (Llewellyn Gross Row, Peterson & Co., New York, 1959)

4 ON THE LIBERAL DEFINITION OF THE SOUTH AFRICAN SITUATION

Hamish Dickie-Clark

Over thirty-five years ago Alfred Hoernlé, a founder of present-day liberalism in South Africa, wrote that liberalism was under attack and 'on the decline all over the world' (1939, p. 103). Recently Leo Kuper, who in his life and work has faced and striven with what must surely be the most searching of all the challenges to liberalism, wrote that there 'can be little doubt that liberals are not viable in extreme racial conflicts' (1974, p. 266). While liberals themselves have been foretelling their own doom, their opponents on both the Right and Left have made devastating attacks on liberal philosophy, policies and tactics. The list of alleged failures and weaknesses is long and varied and much of the criticism seems to be weighty and correct. However, the same could be said of each of the other major political philosophies and it no more disposes of them and their adherents than it does of liberalism and liberals. Moreover, not only do committed liberal scholars like Hoernlé and Kuper go on, despite their prophecies, to call for a revision of traditional liberal approaches, but also others, who do not see themselves as liberals, nevertheless incorporate liberal elements in their policies and actions whether they know and like it or not.

This justifies yet another attempt to understand why liberals are under attack and, more specifically, why, after a promising beginning and despite sustained efforts to meet tremendous demands at the end, liberalism was almost completely overwhelmed in South Africa. Liberals themselves have always been among the first to call for and undertake reassessments of their doctrine and political situation (Hoernlé, 1939; Kuper, 1974; and Robertson, 1971, pp. 106-28, 184-203). Liberal blueprints have always been highly rational, consistent and attractive statements of how people might live in peace and harmony once certain changes have been made. Much less prominent in liberal re-thinking is any attempt to investigate the underlying assumptions made in liberal philosophy about the nature of man and his knowledge of society. The chief aim of this paper is to suggest that here lie some of the reasons why liberalism failed and what further changes would need to be made before it could again make a decisive contribution to the solution of conflict in Southern Africa.

The Liberal Definition

South African liberalism could be for our purposes adequately identified as the attempt to solve the problems of racial conflict by creating interracial solidarity and cooperation on the basis of equal rights and shared values and goals. The official stance of the Liberal Party, created in 1953, included a commitment to non-violence which was upheld by all liberals, with the exception of a handful towards the end of the Party's legal existence. In other matters such as the qualified franchise and the recognition of boycotts and passive resistance as legitimate, there were considerable shifts in opinion among liberals, as they strove to meet changing conditions.

Furthermore, not all liberal-minded people were in the Liberal Party. For many years a decreasing number remained in the white United Party and, at least until its banning in 1960, the African National Congress was decidedly liberal in many of its aims and policies. The Progressive Party, although it is to the right of the disbanded Liberal Party, contains many liberal members. Thus there is still a loosely-defined 'liberal presence' in South Africa. It might even be argued that if one accepts the Hoernlé view that complete separation could be seen as a liberal solution to the race problem, then even some white and black nationalists have been affected by liberal thinking.

Nevertheless, the course of events since the turn of the century shows little sign of being affected by liberal ideals. Indeed the career of liberalism in South Africa makes it easy to question whether such ideals ever had much relevance outside the Cape and after the middle of the nineteenth century. Despite the energetic efforts of able and devoted individuals, some of whom were in positions of considerable power and influence, liberalism came to be increasingly ignored or condemned as merely confusing the 'real' issues.

In trying to account for this, it is clear that the kind of situation which reduces liberalism to impotence is the almost completely polarised one in which nearly all cleavage runs along a single axis and in which your enemy on one front is likely to be your enemy on all other fronts. It is a situation in which that venerable but vicious shibboleth 'He who is not with me is against me' applies with all its destructive force. Then, only total commitment to one side or the other is acceptable or even possible. Conflicts of this inflexible kind arise, as do all social situations, in part from objective factors such as the conquest of one group by another and the particular economic and social conditions which prevail. In part, such situations are created by the people in them defining them as ones which demand total commitment and the use of violence to bring about change. Before going on to the main task of discussing the effect of some of the socially created assumptions underlying liberal philosophy, certain of the more obvious reasons for its ineffectiveness need to be pointed out.

First, it would seem that liberalism was not relevant in the two crucial contests that have been and are still being waged. In the predominantly military phase of the struggle between black and white over the land, it had no part. Later, during the first half of the twentieth century liberalism did have considerable influence on black leaders educated at missionary institutions. But this influence has been steadily reduced until at the present time the real contest would seem to be between the black nationalists and the Marxists to the virtual exclusion of liberals.

I believe that an important reason for the inability of liberalism to have any impact on the black/white struggle outside the Cape and after 1850 is one which is often overlooked. That is the brute fact that the dispossession and continued exploitation of the original inhabitants was too easily and too effectively done and was also too rewarding to be foregone by the white invaders no matter who they were. There can be few, if any, other situations where the rewards were so rich, so lasting and so easily to be had. In such circumstances, it is unlikely that the whites would be impressed either by liberal forebodings or fears of such patently helpless blacks. Indeed such circumstances would mightily reinforce the appeal of the existing ethnocentric world view of the majority of the whites and thus supply them with a satisfactory justification of what they were doing and make them almost immune to the arguments of liberalism.

This is, perhaps, also the reason why, in the struggles within the white group between the supporters of a broader 'South Africanism', as advocated by Botha and Smuts, and a narrower Afrikaner nationalism, liberalism had no say. Its rival ideologies, racism and nationalism, simply left it no room.

Against this background, a number of vital decisions made by liberals can be seen as further causes of their virtual exclusion. Among these would be their principled rejection of even the threat of violence; their refusal to cooperate more fully with the African National Congress because of the latter's acceptance of white communists in the Congress of Democrats; their delay in abandoning the principle of the qualified franchise and in recognising boycotts and passive resistance as legitimate forms of protest. Add to these specific issues the liberal's general inability to take sides in a highly polarised situation, his limitation to rational argument and his lack of enthusiasm for national groupings, and it becomes clear how liberals were virtually shut out from the practical politics of the country.

If such is the kind of intractable conflict situation which makes liberalism ineffective and irrelevant, then the question becomes that of what it was in South African liberalism itself which made it unable to respond to the needs of a multiracial settler society? In what follows I wish to argue that much liberal thinking and tactics in South Africa and elsewhere is founded on a faulty view of the nature of the social world and thus also of the kind of knowedge we can have of it. Moreover, that this overall 'positivistic' or materialist bias has misled liberals into holding, often with paradoxical rigidity and absolutism, specific views about individual human nature which no longer make up the whole or most relevant part of our knowledge of human beings.

Given the elements of 'empiricist' and 'materialistic' thinking in the view of what constitutes 'scientific' knowledge among the English-speaking peoples, it is to be expected that liberals, in Britain, South Africa and other one-time British possessions especially, would have a decided positivistic bias in their approach to the nature of the social world and to our knowledge of it (Arblaster, 1972, pp. 89-91; Hoover, 1975, pp. 88, 109). This has meant that liberals have often taken too much of our knowledge of the world and of human nature as given, even absolute. In this sense it hasn't been idealistic enough and has not been prepared to allow for the extent to which people, in different circumstances and from different ideological standpoints, define their own situation and construct their own reality.

Thus the liberal has tended to assume that too much of the world out there is fixed, amenable to logic, fundamentally rational and open to persuasion. Moreover, that there are certain truths about people which are eternal and absolute, e.g. that they love and strive after freedom under all circumstances. It is surely due to these assumptions that a certain paradoxical doctrinaire stance appears among some liberals which they share with Marxists, perhaps because of their common love of high-level generalisations. But it is more important, in the South African situation at least, that this assumption is clearly what lies behind the liberals' rejection of violence, of radical socialism and of nationalism which has excluded them from effective politics in that country.

More specifically, there would seem to be ways in which the liberal view of the individual's needs may be inadequate. Arblaster (1972) for example has trenchantly criticised liberal individualism which sees the individual person as 'self-propelling, self-contained, and responsible for his own values' and as 'an isolated, non-social (if not actually antisocial) being' whose paramount need is for that freedom which would enable him to fulfil his individuality.

It may well be this view of the individual which explains, in part, liberalism's under-evaluation of the appeal of nationalism. The individual's need for fraternity as well as liberty and equality, his desire to identify himself as a member of a group and to cooperate with others like him, seems to have been seriously underrated by South African liberals. That liberalism has been most readily accepted among the more educated and, therefore, those who are most likely to feel part of an international *Weltbürgertum*, suggests that liberals have less need than others for feeling they belong to their immediate national or other groups. Hoover (1975, pp. 106-62), when discussing the political implications of Erikson's and Skinner's work in psychology, argues that, while Skinner has demonstrated the fact of human conditioning, this does not exclude the possibility of some people's escaping conditioning at least in part, if not wholly. However, to base an ethics on this possibility is to exclude all those who have been conditioned (p. 131). Similarly, Hoover says that Erikson's view of identity, in so far as it is measured by conformity, can vary from near complete conformity to the immediate group all the way to conforming to only a selected few individuals who need not be in even the same place or time (pp. 134-5). I suggest that, in some such way, liberalism has come to regard as universal certain human needs and characteristics which, in fact, are displayed only by the 'detribalised' and fortunate few whose circumstances have enabled them to do so. Thus liberalism's assumptions about the nature of human individuals have made it wholly unattractive and unacceptable to those in South Africa and elsewhere who have a need for some kind of national or group identity of a secular kind.

Another aspect of the same set of assumptions may provide a clue as to why, apart from their undemocratic character, liberalism rejects communism and the more radical forms of socialism. This has to do with the question of whether there is any tension or incompatibility between freedom of the individual and the goal of equality for all, however these key terms may be defined. The question is fundamental in the larger argument over the need to abandon liberty in order to make possible rapid industrialisation and/or decolonisation in postrevolutionary situations. The debate is an old one and one of the earlier versions of it is to be found in Georg Simmel's discussion of the individual and society in the eighteenth century and nineteenth century view of life (1917, Ch. 4). Simmel held that the eighteenth century view

The Liberal Definition

of individuality, by setting up a kind of generalised 'essential' man, stripped of all that he did not have in common with others, was able to reconcile individual freedom and equality but thereby reduced equality to little more than sameness (Wolff's translation 1950, pp. 64-73). In the nineteenth century, according to Simmel, there developed, on the one hand, equality without freedom which Simmel equates with socialism and, on the other, freedom without equality which he calls 'the new individualism'. From the latter standpoint, the individual wants freedom in order to 'distinguish himself *from other individuals*' and, as Simmel goes on to say, the 'important point no longer was the fact that he was a free individual as such, but that he was this specific, irreplaceable, given individual' (Wolff, 1950, p. 78).

While it would be oversimple and incorrect to identify liberal individualism with this 'new individualism' of the nineteenth century only, I would argue that there is more than a little of this kind of freedom without equality in the liberal approach to individual liberty and that it explains, at least partially, the tension between freedom and equality and therefore also the antagonism between liberalism and socialism. Simmel contended that the distinction between equality without freedom and freedom without equality was fundamental and that the principles of economic theory and practice — competition and the division of labour — are expressions of this difference (ibid., pp. 83-4). Moreover,

> There will always be a type of person whose notions regarding social values are contained in the idea of equality of all, however nebulous and unthinkable in the concrete this idea may be. And there will also be a type to whom individual differences and distances constitute an ultimate irreducible and self-justified valued of the social form of existence (ibid. 73-4).

Value judgements such as these are assumptions about the basic nature of human beings which are impervious to rational argument or experimental demonstration and one can choose between them only on the grounds of their emotional attractiveness.

There remains one more aspect of liberal assumptions about individual human nature which is worthy of inclusion. It follows from the notion that the aim of individual freedom is to enable the individual to fulfill himself and that in doing so he best realises the common good of all men. T.H. Green (quoted by Hoover, 1975, pp.39-40) held that freedom was 'the maximum of power for all members of human society able to make the best of themselves.'[1] This very abstract formulation is wholly admirable but begs the question of what 'making the best' of ourselves in some concrete, historical situation may actually involve. According to Hoover (1975, p. 101) Freud held out 'normality' as the overall human aim; Mead called for 'adjustment'; Skinner for 'survival' and Erikson for 'identity'. As they must be, all of these are rather general concepts, but their protagonists do give them more specific shape when arguing for them. Moreover, there would seem to be considerable evidence that these are among the things which people want and need in varying measure depending on their circumstances.

Is it not possible to arrive at a similar list of what various groups in concrete situations want or think they want? For instance, in South Africa at different times both Afrikaners and Africans have wanted desperately to relieve the bitterness of defeat and oppression by establishing themselves as distinct from those they saw as their enemies. Or, are there not, perhaps, times in the life of groups when equality is to be preferred to individual freedom? Is it not conceivable that the liberal spirit could abandon some of its cherished assumptions about human nature and with them something of its uncompromising ethics of conviction (*Gesinnungsethik*)? Unless it finds some way of doing so, it may be fated to remain helpless and unwanted on the sidelines of the political field in those very countries which most need what it could offer.

Notes

I am grateful to Heribert Adam and Keith Dixon for their useful comments on this chapter.

1. In passing one could point out that Green's acceptance of freedom being power to do certain things comes close to Simmel's definition of freedom as dependent on our power over others. This also suggests another reason why freedom and equality might be incompatible.

References

Arblaster, A. 'Liberal Values and Socialist Values,' *The Socialist Register* (1972), pp. 83-104

Hoernlé, R.F.A. *South African Native Policy and the Liberal Spirit* (University of Cape Town, Cape Town, 1939)

Hoover, K.R. *A Politics of Identity* (University of Illinois Press, Urbana, Chicago, London, 1975)

Kuper, Leo *Race, Class and Power* (Duckworth, London, 1974)
Robertson, Janet *Liberalism in South Africa, 1948-1963* (Clarendon Press, London, 1971)
Simmel, Georg *Grundfragen der Soziologie* (Berlin & Leipzig, 1917), (English translation in Kurt Wolff's *The Sociology of Georg Simmel*) (Free Press, Glencoe, 1950)

5 THE IMPOSSIBILITY OF A LIBERAL SOLUTION IN SOUTH AFRICA

Pierre L. van den Berghe

The white regimes of Southern Africa are now entering the final convulsions of their violent history. Their end, long predicted but hitherto delayed by force, represents the last chapter in the book of European colonialism in Africa. Despite their claim to indigenous status, the four million whites of Southern Africa are in imminent danger of being forced to emigrate. They have failed either to assimilate themselves to the Africans, or to assimilate the latter to them. Blacks are increasingly unwilling to tolerate them as an alien and privileged enclave, even in a residual little 'Whitestan'. Whites are, for the most part, unwilling to stay on terms other than privilege. The stark alternatives are indefinite warfare and chaos with the constant threat of death, or emigration. Nearly thirty years of apartheid have led to their logical conclusion, racial polarisation. There is no room left for compromise. Open, violent conflict seems inevitable.

Had South Africa adopted, even as late as 20 or 25 years ago, the course suggested by liberals, a viable, democratic, non-racial society might still have been possible. The liberals had an eminently sane, rational, just and ethical vision for South Africa; unfortunately, they remained a voice in the wilderness.[1] The Liberal Party at its height had some 7,000 members, including some 3,000, mostly university-educated, whites. A couple of hundred whites espoused positions to the left of the Liberal Party, and substantially larger numbers of whites flirted with the Progressive Party to the right of the 'universal franchise' liberals, but even by a wide definition of liberalism that would include the Progressive Party, its appeal was limited to at most five per cent of the white population. Among Coloureds and Indians, liberalism had a certain emotional and moral appeal, but it never gained any kind of mass following. The Coloured community (except for a few intellectuals) stayed largely out of radical opposition politics. In the Indian group, the South African Indian Congress, founded by Mahatma Gandhi, had a long and distinguished history, and its ideology was very close to that of the Liberal Party, but it competed with the conservative Natal Indian Organisation, and neither group achieved a genuine mass following.

The Impossibility of a Liberal Solution

The relationship of liberalism and the Liberal Party to the Africans was more complex. Until the early 1960s, the mission-educated, Christian leadership of the African National Congress, by far the biggest and best organised radical opposition group in South Africa, and represented by such people as A.B. Xuma, Z.K. Matthews and Albert Luthuli, espoused a broadly liberal ideology. To be sure, South African liberalism was different in several respects from its nineteenth century European counterpart, and included a strong Gandhian influence, but this was equally true of the African National Congress and the Liberal Party. Liberalism, then, had considerable appeal to urban Africans and even in the more westernised sectors of the peasantry, as shown by the broad and nearly uncontested appeal of the African National Congress, and by considerable African attendance at public meetings of the Liberal Party.

Starting in the late 1950s, however, younger and more radical leaders arose within the African National Congress and its Youth League. One group was supported by the South African Communist Party, operating through the all-white Congress of Democrats, and through its African and Indian members in the Congress Alliance. It attacked liberalism as petty bourgeois reformism in defence of the interests of English capitalism. Another wing, which gave birth to the splinter Pan African Congress, opposed both communism and liberalism. It saw both as dominated by white intellectuals, and advocated an exclusive black nationalist policy. In view of the repression of both the ANC and PAC by the South African Government in the 1960s, it is difficult to say which of the two movements commands mass support, but the sporadic unrest of the 1970s, and especially, the events of 1976 indicate considerable support for a black nationalism that would exclude whites. The days of the 1950s when passive resistance campaigns and boycotts could rally some small measure of multiracial participation seem past. Liberalism began as marginal to white politics, but as a strong ideological current in African opposition politics. In the last decade or two, it has become increasingly irrelevant to both.

The question is: why did the political ideology and moral posture most likely in the abstract to give all South Africans a viable future on the basis of equal rights and human dignity fail to gain appreciable support in any group? Why did it fail to make any perceptible impact on the course of events? Why did hundreds of eminently articulate, rational, courageous, humane, honest, and moral people fail to make a dent in the South African madhouse?

The facile answer is of course: because South Africa is such an insane society. This is true enough, but does not tell us a great deal. Besides, not only in South Africa are reason and justice irrelevant to the solution of social conflicts, especially of communal conflicts. The failure of South African liberalism is, alas, laden with universal lessons. As Leo Kuper, the embodiment of South African liberalism at its best, so despairingly documents in his recent comparative study of revolution in Algeria, Zanzibar, Rwanda and Burundi, the voice of reason, decency and universalism is smothered in the escalating clamour of sectionalism and the polarisation of violence and counter-violence (Kuper, 1977).

A more complex and instructive answer requires at least four levels of analysis. Starting with the most general level, communalism in its multifarious strains (tribalism, nationalism, ethnocentrism, racism, sectarianism, and so on) may well have a genetic basis. Modern sociobiology is discovering that in a wide array of species, from social insects to primates, and including man, organisms behave in ways that favour not only their own survival but that of other organisms that are genetically related to them (Barash, 1977; Wilson, 1975). 'Inclusive fitness' or 'kin selection' theory says, in effect, that the evolutionary game calls for passing on one's genes, either directly through one's own reproduction, or indirectly through the reproduction of kin who share genes with one. Thus, one can expect that the degree of biological relatedness will be a good predictor of cooperative (or, conversely, conflictual and aggressive) behaviour.[2]

Nearly all 'natural' human communities — those wherein one is born, one marries, one reproduces and one dies — define membership in terms of kinship or blood, either directly or indirectly. This may be expressed through a variety of cultural idioms (e.g. a common religion or a common language), and the kinship may be putative rather than real, but the community is largely conceived as an extended family linked by ties of 'blood'. The leader is a 'father' to his 'children', members are 'brothers' and 'sisters' to each other. Those outside the group are antithetically defined as people (if, indeed, one goes as far as granting them humanity at all) with whom one shares little or nothing in common. Of all the bases for establishing human communities, the most fraught with explosive conflict is probably race. This is true, not because race corresponds to a biologically meaningful distinction — indeed, racial distinctions are biologically trivial — but because they are thought to be biologically significant and often provide a physical badge of instantaneous recognition. Skin pigmentation, or relative lack of it, is perhaps the crudest but the most visible badge of group membership.

This biological reductionism is bound to be repulsive to most social scientists raised in a tradition of cultural determinism. Of course it does not explain everything, for human behaviour is determined by a complex blend of biological, ecological and socio-cultural factors. However, cultural determininists are always at a loss to explain the monotonous ferociousness, the blind hatred and irrationality, and the instantaneously contagious emotionality of communal conflicts. A trivial and accidental stimulus, interpreted rightly or wrongly as a provocation, can, with lightning rapidity, escalate into a communal conflict totally out of proportion with the initial incident. Violence continues unabated even when it is obvious to many participants that no one benefits by it. Pure spite prevails until violence is suppressed by the greater organised violence of the state, until one party wipes out the other, or until both parties have decimated each other into exhaustion. Communal conflicts simply defy rationality. Surely, there must be a biological basis to our 'gut reactions'.[3]

At this most general biological level, it is clear that the ideology of liberalism, based as it is on universalistic values, can make very little appeal in communal conflicts. Fundamental to liberalism is the rejection of all group distinctions; liberty, equality and fraternity are indivisible and apply to all, irrespective of race, religion, or ethnicity. It is interesting that the equally universalistic ideology of socialism based on the highly rational notion of class interest across communal and national boundaries meets with an equally resounding lack of success in societies like South Africa, where class lines cut across communal lines. Indeed, the slogan of the South African Communist Party during the Witwatersrand white miners' strike of 1922 was 'Workers of the world, unite and fight for a white South Africa.'

A second level at which to analyse the failure of South African liberalism is in terms of the tendency for conflicts to polarise. In the 1950s and 1960s, the Liberal Party represented roughly the extreme left of white opinion, the centre for Coloured and Indian opinion, and the centre-right of African opinion.[4] As such, it represented a genuine common ground — narrow and tenuous though that ground was — cutting across racial lines. It was in fact, along with the Communists, the only organised political group whose membership approached in racial composition the general population. Many students of revolutionary change, and most recently Leo Kuper (1977), have noted that the middle ground becomes increasingly untenable as the conflict unfolds, and remains so until it has run its course (at which time it often becomes irrelevant to the new, changed situation).

Liberals were, of course, anathema to the overwhelming bulk of both Afrikaners and English-speaking South Africans, and to the Nationalist and United Parties which respectively represented these groups. Liberalism not only attacked head on all the ideological premises of racism and segregation; it also attacked the very legitimacy and ethical foundations of South African society. It was the uncomfortable voice of conscience which faced whites with the alternative of rejecting its premises as idealistic and unpractical, or accepting them and feeling guilty. Understandably, nearly all whites opted for the first course.

Liberalism might have been expected to appeal to Coloureds and Indians, two minority groups in an intermediary position in the South African racial hierarchy. To a limited extent it did, at the level of the educated leadership, but it failed to attract the masses of these groups. Until recently, most Coloureds were, in fact, hoping for assimilation in the privileged white group rather than an abolition of the system of racial discrimination for everybody. As for Indians, many feared that the Liberal Party platform of universal franchise would lead *de facto* to an anti-Indian black government. Post-independence events in East Africa, especially in Uganda, have done nothing to allay Indian fears of African government.

The reactions of Africans to liberalism were also ambivalent. After the Liberal Party adopted the principle of universal adult suffrage, its platform was almost identical with that of the African National Congress, and its Gandhian ideology of non-violence and passive resistance appealed to the older, mission-educated generation of the African Congress leadership. However, African ideology became increasingly radicalised in the early 1960s. The surprising thing is not that African opinion radicalised, but that it was so slow and reluctant to do in the face of increasingly brutal repression. In any case, during the last years before the Liberal Party and the ANC were forced underground, their relations were officially polite and mutually respectful, but ambivalently so on the ANC's side. The Liberal Party was increasingly seen, at least by the communist-influenced leadership, as a coterie of well-meaning white intellectuals, marginal to the liberation struggle. At the mass level, it made virtually no impact, except briefly in some urban centres like Durban and Capetown.

A third level of failure of South African liberalism concerns white politics and interests. Liberalism was first and foremost a desperate appeal to South African whites to change their attitudes towards non-whites. The appeal was made on both moral and pragmatic grounds. Racialism was ethically indefensible, said the liberals. In this they were

The Impossibility of a Liberal Solution

supported by much of the Anglican and Catholic high clergy, and roundly denounced by the Dutch Reformed Churches. Arguments surrounding the morality or immorality of apartheid were thus reduced to a minor theme in a continuing political debate following highly predictable alignments. It did not, apparently, change many minds, much less hearts.

Further, said the liberals, racism and apartheid were not only morally bankrupt. They also threatened the long-range interests of the whites; they jeopardised white survival in Southern Africa by fostering racial hatred against the whites, and by provoking the inevitable revolution that would overthrow them not only as political overlords, but even as a people with a right to live in the area. The point of no return for compromise and adaptation to the winds of change was quickly approaching, warned the liberals with anguished urgency in the 1950s and the early 1960s.

Points of no return are notoriously difficult to determine, except in retrospect. Perhaps Sharpeville was one. In any case, the argument cut both ways; for, if the point of no return was already reached when the warnings were sounded, then it made good sense for the whites to retrench in the *laager* for the final struggle. Rigid, *verkrampte* apartheid was perhaps the most rational way of postponing the racial bloodbath, while concessions and compromises would merely accelerate the demise of the whites.

The one major element in the South African situation which liberals, and more generally, most political analysts have often underrated is the rationality and internal consistency of the South African albinocracy in pursuing the perpetuation of its privileged position. South African whites have erected a political structure aimed at preserving a vast and complex edifice of privilege which simply cannot survive even moderate, gradualist change along the lines of free enterprise capitalism and neo-colonialism. The problem is thus quite different from that of other white minorities in tropical Africa, and more akin to that of the French settlers in Algeria. What is at stake in South Africa is not simply the skin pigmentation of political office holders. Neo-colonial countries like Ivory Coast or Kenya have shown that white minorities have taken such change easily in their stride, and that whites often find themselves in a more comfortable position than they were before independence. They reap the fuits of exploitation without the burden of political responsibility.

The crux of the matter in South Africa, however, is that the whites have created an economic system so grossly at variance with a free market and have erected so many protective walls for their economic privileges, that even a relatively conservative change in the direction of a capitalist, neo-colonial economy would severely undermine the standard of living of perhaps two-thirds to three-fourths of the white population. The incredible split labour market of South Africa, for instance, ensures a white worker a rate of pay from four to ten times higher than that attainable by an equally skilled black worker. The Chamber of Mines and the large capitalist interest groups of South Africa could easily weather the storm of a political transfer to black rule. Indeed, after a temporary disruption, South African capital might be better off than under apartheid for being able to get rid of grossly overpaid white workers. But the mass of the white population cannot countenance even a transfer of power to a conservative black regime. Such a transfer would mean a drastic reduction in the artificially high white standard of living; so drastic, in fact, that emigration to Canada, Australia, New Zealand or the United States would seem an irresistibly attractive alternative.[5]

White emigration, I am convinced, is the most desirable and humane solution to the Southern African problem. Unlike Asian Africans who were reluctantly admitted to Europe and America and faced numerous prejudices after resettlement, white Africans can expect both easy acceptance and adaptation to high standard of living countries similar in culture to what they have known in Africa. Other than replacing their house servants with vacuum cleaners and washing machines, they will have few adjustments to make. The more whites emigrate and the sooner, the better for South Africa. Then, perhaps, the few whites who are willing to stay on terms of equality with blacks will be able to remain in Africa.

If my analysis is correct, however, the seemingly obstinate and irrational behaviour of the South African and Rhodesian regimes becomes comprehensible. They correctly perceive that there can be no compromise, no middle road between apartheid and an integrated, non-racial society. Concessions on the part of the white regimes can only lead to the devolution of power to a majority government, hence to the loss of white political and economic privileges. Change has been delayed so long that even the prospects for a slow, orderly transition are slender. Any substantial change at this stage would open the floodgates. It is, therefore, totally unrealistic to expect the white regimes to do anything but stand pat, except under the threat of foreign intervention

The liberal premise, therefore, that the deracialisation of South African society was in everybody's long-term interests, while certainly

The Impossibility of a Liberal Solution

correct in the nineteenth century and perhaps as late as the Second World War, increasingly ceased to be realistic and credible in the last two or three decades. The madness inherent in apartheid leaves no room for compromise or adaptation. Apartheid can be bolstered only by coercion and violence, else it must collapse utterly. Nor did liberal arguments about the cost of maintaining apartheid cut much ice with its proponents and architects. The costs of apartheid in terms of repressive apparatus and loss of productivity, not to mention human misery, are, to be sure, staggering. But they are overwhelmingly borne by blacks. To nearly all whites, the benefits of apartheid greatly overshadow the marginal inconveniences (such as military service). Only open, large-scale insurrection by blacks will alter that cost-benefit ratio for whites. Only then, and under additional foreign pressures, can the white regimes be expected to budge. It is under this kind of pressure that Vorster decided by 1975 that Namibia and Zimbabwe were lost causes, and hence that their white minorities were expendable in the interest of defending the central South African *laager*.

Liberalism, in short, failed to appeal to South African whites at the rational level, at the moral level, and at the 'gut' biological level. The universalistic rationality of liberalism confronted the logic of apartheid which, once it had created a social system around its premises, developed a perverse rationality of its own.

Finally, the failure of liberalism can be analysed in terms of class interest theory, namely that liberalism was the ideology of a class that was too narrow to have an appreciable impact on the society at large, or even on its ruling albinocracy. One version of this argument was the one advanced by a few South African Marxists in the Congress of Democrats and the sadly misnamed Unity Movement. According to them, liberalism was the ideology of English capitalism. That thesis could gain plausibility only by stretching the definition of liberalism to include the Progressive Party and even the United Party. These two parties were, and still are, the political embodiment of English capital in South Africa, but the United Party is hardly liberal even by the broadest definition, and the Progressive Party is a reembodiment of nineteenth century Cape Liberalism with a strong dash of paternalism.

At no time did the Liberal Party — the only organised political group in South Africa that represented genuine liberalism — receive significant support from the English business community. If any class label is to be attached to the Liberal Party, it was the party of the intelligentsia. It drew most of its tenuous support from university lecturers and students, lawyers, clergymen, schoolteachers, writers, and journalists, that is overwhelmingly salaried or free professionals rather than businessmen.[6] A few of its members were relatively wealthy, but a good many were poor African farmers as well. It was disproportionately, but not overwhelmingly, white; in fact, whites made up only some 40 per cent of the membership, and Indians were also overrepresented. Among its white members, the vast bulk were English-speaking, but the Party also attracted a sprinkling of young Afrikaner intellectuals.

Certainly, the Liberal Party did cut across racial, confessional and ethnic lines more than any other political group in South Africa except for the communists. It was first and foremost a party of the intelligentsia, and therein lay one of the several reasons for its limited appeal. Its consistently high level of intellectual discourse, its meticulous analysis of the evils of South African society, its pleas for rationality were not geared at mass appeal, although at one stage it did have some African peasant following in Natal.

While it is inaccurate to describe liberalism and the Liberal Party as the embodiment of English capitalism in South Africa, there is, however, a sense in which Marxian class analysis applies to the recruitment of liberals. Few of them stood to lose by the enactment of the program they advocated. This is especially true of white liberals. The Party had few farmers threatened by the prospect of land reform, few artisans or petty clerks threatened with job displacement by qualified blacks, and a great many intellectuals and professionals, relatively secure in their academic jobs, their higher education, and their expertise. White liberals were, for the most part, those people best equipped to retain a secure place in South Africa, almost irrespective of political regime (short of an Idi Amin, of course). For the reasons already mentioned, white liberals thus represented a small minority of the white population.

It may be argued that white professionals, academics and technicians also benefit from apartheid through the artificial elimination of non-white competition, and, indeed, this is the case. Most whites in these categories never did support the liberal cause. My argument is merely that, of the whites, those with a university-level education have relatively least to fear from the universalistic, non-racial policies advocated by the liberals, and that, therefore, liberalism appeals mostly to that small sector of the white population. To be sure, admission to higher education in South Africa is racially selective, but it is also elitist along class lines. Even the elimination of all racial discrimination would still leave white intellectuals with a strong competitive advantage for a couple of generations, if only because of the accumulated bonus of past

The Impossibility of a Liberal Solution

racial discrimination. The pure meritocracy advocated by many liberals thus poses little direct threat to the white intelligentsia, but an obvious and immediate threat to most South African whites in manual, farming or petty clerical occupations.

White intellectuals also do quite well by apartheid, if they are prepared to accept restrictions on their civil liberties and academic freedom. However, liberals among them see liberalism as a morally and practically appealing alternative to either black nationalism or revolutionary socialism. The former would discriminate against them on racial grounds, and the latter on class grounds. Liberalism, whether it is consciously perceived as such or not, is a meritocratic ideology peculiarly congenial to the class interests of the intelligentsia. A liberal revolution in South Africa would relieve the white intellectual of the moral burden imposed by racially ascribed privilege without appreciably endangering his class position in his own or his children's lifetime. Objectively, this is the best bargain which any white can strike anywhere in the Africa of the 1970s.

This view of white liberalism in South Africa is not to be construed as saying that white liberals were calculating, Machiavellian, self-serving powermongers. Indeed, many of them were perspicacious enough to have an acute sense of the futility of their political action. Many were also remarkably courageous and disinterested people willing to face harassment, exile, arrest, detention and loss of a job for their convictions. Liberalism was never a comfortable stance to take, except in an abstract moral sense. But their vision of the future was one that would have served them well. At the same time, with no prospect of coming to power, or even of sharing it, liberals could and did remain uncompromisingly true to their ideology.

Is liberalism, then, more than a noble but Quixotic footnote to South African history, a sad morality tale in a rotten, oppressive society? I think the answer is yes. Oppression is a powerful catalyst for human depravity, but also for decency. Like the Soviet dissidents whom they resemble in many ways, South African liberals come off remarkably well. They belong to the rare breed of people who keep us from despairing about the human condition. Theirs was a glorious failure. Indeed, the failure was not theirs, but the system's. The liberal ideal remains viable; it was the nature of South African society that made its implementation impossible.

Notes

1. Among the numerous sources by and/or about South African liberals, see Kuper (1960, 1965); Marquard (1960, 1962); Paton (1948, 1953, 1958); Robertson (1971).
2. This is not the place to expand on the implications of sociobiology for an understanding of human social behaviour. The reader will find a short introduction in Barash (1977) and a longer one in Wilson (1975). For some of my own writings on the subject, see van den Berghe (1974, 1979), and van den Berghe and Barash (1977).
3. In earlier publications (van den Berghe, 1958, 1967, 1970) I differentiated between what I called a 'paternalistic' and a 'competitive' type of race relations, but without linking the typology to sociobiology. Now, I am convinced that the fundamental difference between the two types is that in the paternalistic type (of which the slave plantation is a prototype) the racial groups do not constitute communities as they do in competitive situations. The slave plantation itself is a multiracial community, albeit of a very special type, in which the racial groups interbreed extensively; therefore race relations are bound to be radically different from the situation of the contemporary United States or South Africa, where communal lines coincide largely with racial lines and where racial endogamy is almost total.
4. This formulation is an oversimplification, for the diverse range of political opinions in South Africa is not easily reducible to a single continuum of right to left. Nonetheless, the Liberal Party was drawing rather conservative Africans and daringly radical whites. If any group could have been said to occupy the centre of the political stage, the Liberal Party was it.
5. In support of the validity of my analysis is the fact that the South African and Rhodesian regimes have already imposed stringent restrictions on the export of capital to prevent whites from emigrating. Whites who opt to leave must now leave behind most of their assets.
6. While the Liberal Party drew disproportionately from the highly educated and articulate, the reciprocal is not true: most intellectuals did not belong to the Liberal Party.

References

Barash, David P. *Sociobiology and Behavior* (Elsevier, New York, 1977)
Kuper, Leo *Passive Resistance in South Africa* (Yale University Press, New Haven, 1960)
——, *An African Bourgeoisie* (Yale University Press, New Haven, 1965)
——, *The Pity of It All: Polarization of Racial and Ethnic Relations*, (Duckworth, London, 1977)
Marquand, Leo *The Story of South Africa* (Faber and Faber, London, 1960)
——, *The Peoples and Policies of South Africa* (Oxford University Press, London, 1962)
Paton, Alan *Cry the Beloved Country* (Scribner, New York, 1948)
——, *Too Late the Phalarope* (Scribner, New York, 1953)
——, *Hope for South Africa* (Pall Mall, London, 1958)
Robertson, Janet *Liberalism in South Africa, 1948-1963* (Clarendon Press, Oxford, 1971)
van den Berghe, Pierre L. 'The Dynamics of Racial Prejudice', *Social Forces*

(1958), 37, pp. 138-141
——, *Race and Racism* (John Wiley, New York, 1967)
——, *Race and Ethnikcity* (Basic Books, New York, 1970)
——, 'Bringing Beasts Back In', *American Sociological Review* (1974), 39, pp. 777-88
——, *Human Family Systems* (Elsevier, New York, 1979)
——, and Barash, David P. 'Inclusive Fitness and Human Family Structure', *American Anthropologist* (1977), 79, pp. 809-23
Wilson, Edward O. *Sociobiology, the New Synthesis* (The Belknap Press, Cambridge, Mass., 1975)

6 SOCIOLOGY AND UNIVERSAL REALITY: SOUTH AFRICAN IMPLICATIONS

Fatima Meer

It is over a hundred years since Auguste Comte pointed the way. Yet our grasp of social reality has never been less sure. The imbalance between man's control of his physical and his social world is so great today that the achievements of the natural sciences are in danger of being annihilated by the deterioration in human relations. What has gone wrong?

The Sociologist: Myth Maker or Realist?

What has gone wrong is that sociology has not functioned as the science of society. It has functioned primarily to rationalise the order of power. We are so far removed from society today, because sociology has conspired to keep us so far removed. Comte and his followers did not develop a science of society, but a technique for defining and upholding the capitalist model as the perfect social order. We, his followers, have so succeeded in equating the capitalist model with 'real' society that it does not occur to us that we might search for reality outside of it. The capitalist society has become society. We study other societies, really non-societies, with a view to making them into societies by bringing them into the capitalist orbit. Having made the capitalist order into the absolute, all other orders have been relegated to the position of temporary relatives.

The use of the natural science method has not so much increased our knowledge of social phenomena as it has legitimated capitalist claims to absolutism. Comte and his successors realised that traditional morality could not legitimate this claim without undoing itself, that it would compel the submission of the new order to its moral test and thereby stifle its progress. Sociology hence undid the claim of moral absolutism and set aside the existing absolute, as perceived by the traditional seers, by Christ, Buddha, Muhammad, Krishna, as non-scientific, beyond human realisation, not of the world known to man. Faith was replaced by pragmatism.

The extension of the physical scientific method to the study of social phenomena replaced the requirement of moral consistency in the evaluation of society with that of functionality, a principle borrowed from organic reality, and foreign to social relations. Society no longer had to be good but simply to function effectively. This relieved industrial society of the restraining effects of moral control and left it free to operate in terms of its own internal rules. Social relations were consequently forced into the organismic and then technological framework, and system analysis became the order of the day.

The one risk mainstream sociologists could not take was to see social relations in the context of *human* relations, a network of interaction within a framework built on absolute values, as propounded by the traditional seers, for this would undermine European industrial society, which they held up as prototypical.

The amoral, neutral stance of sociologists may well be a valid stance in pursuit of scientific objectivity, but it would be naive to see its contribution to unrestrained capitalist exploitation as coincidental. The neutral, amoral, objective stance of social science legitimates capitalist excesses effectively as does the Protestant ethic.

European society is consequently characterised by a blurring of good and evil. European man is certainly unique in his ability to sanctify sin, to convert it into a positive social value. Other men sin, but without moral comfort. Vine Deloria Jr. (1972, p. 189) states that because sins succeed, success is the measure of reality:

> The white man has the marvelous ability to conceptualize. He has also the marvelous inability to distinguish between sacred and profane. He therefore arbitrarily conceptualizes all things and understands none of them. His science creates gimmicks for his use. Little effort is made to relate the gimmicks to the nature of his life or to see them in an historical context.

European Man's Addiction to Myths

European man in effect replaces 'reality' with the myth that he concocts out of it. His pragmatism is nothing more than his insistence on evidence — evidence for the concocted myth. He abandons faith in the existence of the Absolute and settles for Maya. Where, to a Hindu or Muslim, the Sermon on the Mount would be divine in itself, European man must have evidence for it, in the myth of the Resurrection. Christ is God, not because he *is* God, but because of the evidence of the Resurrection, the miracles of the loaves and of Lazarus. He is God not in Himself but through the grace of His pragmatism. While Hinduism is fertile with myths, the myths do not substantiate reality — they illustrate it.

Comte conceived sociology as the new Christianity, but sociology could not replace Christianity, because, among other things, it proved to be less pragmatic than Christianity. It did not even study society, but the idea of society. It promised a perfect society — and no perfect society is in the offing. Christianity, more realistic, defines an ongoing conflict between good and evil and promises heaven only after death.

The mainstream view of society keeps close to the Comtean myth that 'society is a harmony of structure and function working towards a common end through action and reaction', that 'social progress is marked by an increasing specialisation of functions and a corresponding tendency toward an adaptation and perfection of organs', that 'social disturbances are maladies of the social organism', that superordinate and subordinate roles are 'natural and spontaneous', that 'while there is a universal desire to command, it is no less essential to observe that people find it very agreeable to throw the burden of expert guidance upon others' (quoted in Becker and Barnes, 1952, pp. 571-88).

The principle of human inequality, conflicting as it does with the concept of the brotherhood of man, probably stimulates most research in the social sciences, and sociologists are pushed into offering the most obtuse rhetoric, to state that the poor are poor because they want to be poor. Thus Hyman (1953, p. 425) states:

> there are other factors of a more subtle psychological nature . . . it is our assumption that an intervening variable mediating the relationship between low positions and lack of upward mobility is a system of beliefs and values within the lower classes which in turn reduces the very *voluntary* actions which would ameliorate their low position.
>
> . . . To put it simply the lower class individual doesn't want as much success, he knows he couldn't get it even if he wanted to, and doesn't want what might help him get success. His value system creates a *self-imposed* barrier.

The educated by contrast are described as

> not so aggressive or obvious in achieving or maintaining success. They trust in people and are thus able to develop long term relationships that aid their careers, particularly in bureaucratic structures where the judgment of peers is so critical. They put efficiency ahead of nepotism. They believe in planning and are prepared to move away from parents (Kahl, 1965).

The injury thus done to the poor is all the more reprehensible for the fact that their stigmatisation bears the authoritative seal of science. One may well imagine too the bewilderment of the poor who know very well why they are poor and are just waiting for the day to get even.

Sociology in South Africa

South African sociologists are perhaps the furthest removed from reality, for they have to contend with not only a fictitious, capitalist absolute, but a fictitious, capitalist, racist absolute. Moreover, they are less free than sociologists in most other countries to analyse this model critically. The repressive political system demands conformity to the point of defining practically any fundamental change as furthering the aims of communism and therefore treason. The silencing of such academics as the Turners, the Simons and Hoffenbergs must operate as a serious deterrent.

South African sociologists are stuck with the apartheid model as the ultimate reality. They devote themselves largely to the teaching of structural functionalism and studying what is, and discreetly keeping away from considerations of what ought to be, dismissing this as unrealistic and idealistic. The danger, however, is that they tend to see what is as what will always be, thereby giving the apartheid system an eternal lease on 'scientific' grounds. Like Comte and Parsons, they accept the ongoing social system in which they find themselves and justify it through the standpoint of ethical neutrality. But at least Parsons' paradigm was culled from a reality in the shaping of which the interacting members had some role. The reality references of South African sociologists is the sheer invention of Afrikaner legislators.

And while they thus limit their field of reality, out in the Black 'underworld' which they dismiss as inconsequential or too dangerous, a whole revolution seethes. They may run around in circles to explain the periodic splutterings, and to suggest how the resultant tears in the system may be mended. But on the whole, they are quite useless and patently without insight. Change, of course, is inevitable in view of South Africa's position in Africa and in the world, but South African sociologists will not predict it, let alone act as midwives.

Sociology, like Christianity, is a western concept to Southern Africa. Both sociology and Christianity are dependent on the sources that finance them and if Christianity, in particular Protestantism, has operated 'innocently' as the right hand of capitalism, then sociology equally 'innocently' has operated as its left hand.

There is little doubt that the history of sociology is a history of intellectual support for the *status quo*, for existing order, and since it is an invention of Western capitalism, it has operated above all to support that order. Martin Nicolaus finds this implicit in the standpoints of both the classical and modern fathers of sociology, of August Comte and Talcott Parsons respectively. Nicolaus (1972, pp. 47-8) says:

> The core of the Comtean vision of society, which was the mission of sociology, using the 'positive' method, to realize, lies in the marriage of modern capitalist-industrial productive forces with the kind of social and political relationships which obtained at the peak of theocratic feudalism. To achieve this end he proposed the establishment, at public expense, of a caste of scientist priests.

Nicolaus goes on to say that Talcott Parsons (1968) confirms this idea when he says: 'The fundamental origin of the modern professional system, then, has lain in the marriage between the academic professional and certain categories of practical men.' Nicolaus (1972, p. 46) emphasises that it is a marriage in which the professions play a subordinate female role and there is an 'institutionalised appropriation by the superior of the subordinate's services, in return for money or commodities'.

Thus stated, sociology as popularly practised is far from an objective instrument for capturing social reality as the positivists see it to be. It is simply a world view, and is no more *the* world view than Christianity is *the* world religion, or capitalism *the* world economic system. Its claim, however, to be the only objective view of human relations is so persuasive that it has practically driven all other world views into their shells and herein lies the real threat of sociology to the fuller understanding of social reality. Unless sociology redefines itself and discards the bourgeois world view that well nigh monopolises it, it will continue to be a partial commentary, on a part of the total social reality. To raise itself to the status of a universal social science it will not only have to recognise other European traditions, as it is now beginning to do, but it will also have to take full account of the intellectual and philosophical traditions of other countries and cultures. Durkheim's collective conscience, and Freud's model of the human personality, based on the 'reality' of the unconscious and his tri-partite structuring of the personality into id, ego and super ego, are no more true than the Hindu theory of Karma and Dharma, or the Hindu concept of personality as configurations of Prakriti (matter) and Atman (soul).

Mental constructs abstracted from the Western social reality are not always applicable to an African or Asian situation, yet these situations continue to be researched and reshaped to correspond to these constructs. This is apparent in the search for and manufacture of a European-type class where in fact no such class exists. It is apparent too in the conceptualisation of caste, where Western trained researchers deeply sensitive to hierarchy see it, above all, as a divisive and hierarchical ordering of rights, privileges and economic functions though caste members themselves experience it primarily as a protective net which ensconces their rights to friendship, marriage, territory, water, and are far more sensitive to its functional, emotional and material consequences than to its depriving ones.

All this has a pertinent bearing on the present condition of sociology in Southern Africa. It has continued to be ethnocentric, continued to be a vocation of practitioners drawn almost exclusively from the ruling group, and it has operated fundamentally on behalf of that group. In other words, it continues to see Southern Africa through white eyes, through white theoretical constructs and through white methodological procedures irrespective of whether the latter two are valid or not. This has serious consequences for the nature and quality of the Southern African social reality it reveals. The urgent question is, to what extent have social scientists been looking at Southern Africa and to what extent have they been looking at Europe looking at Southern Africa?

Sociology in Southern Africa is in the main sociology in South Africa. The distance between black and white is so great that any white social scientist would be deluding himself if he believed that he had succeeded in removing the barrier, that he had succeeded in penetrating the black mind and interpreting black life.

Yet the white social scientist continues to depend almost exclusively upon himself to interpret this reality, persuading himself that the conceptual tools he takes into the field are sufficient in themselves to generate the 'truth'. It may be well to emphasise here that the positivist's claim to the natural science fraternity is based much less on his demonstrated empiricism than on the sheer boom of his rhetoric; that far from being objective in the natural science sense, his method is shot through with cultural relativism; that he subjectively selects his problem, and though ideally he should take into account all social factors affecting it, in fact he cannot do this, and he is obliged to select only those which he considers important. Finally, he observes only a sample of the problem and, for all the precautions he may take to be objective, his selection does not escape his subjective wishes, and this must be assumed to have crucial implications in social research.

Since sociology is the *interpretation* of social factors, not social facts, the interpreter is of crucial importance, and to assume that he is culture or value free is to contradict a fundamental sociological principle, that we are the products of socialisation.

If, then, the intrusion of the subject into the object is inevitable in the study of human relations, then distance between object and subject functions far less in enhancing objectivity, as is often stated in support of non-Africans interpreting African cultures, than identity between object and subject functions to promote the closer understanding of the 'objective reality'.

In the absence of social scientists drawn from the Southern African situation, the social sciences have tended to be used exploitatively in Africa, their main functions being to provide sufficient information for the more effective control and subjugation of the African and to construct an 'African reality' that emphasises his difference and thereby justifies his different treatment. A number of psychologists, using tests structured in a non-African cultural milieu, have 'proved' his inferiority, or demonstrated that he is incapable of matching white performance in a white world. Anthropologists have elevated him into the noble savage, lovable and understandable, but living on a different level of civilisation.

White social scientists who have broken free from this interpretation of the black man have been accused of abandoning their professional commitment to objectivity, and becoming value oriented. The low level of tolerance for radical sociology in the country has been demonstrated in particular by the casualties suffered by the Department of Sociology at the University of Natal. Three of its members felt constrained to leave the country and some of the works of two well-known sociologists, Leo Kuper and Pierre van den Berghe, who worked in the Department, the former as its head, are banned in South Africa.

Martin Shaw (1972) states that 'Sociology is primarily an intellectual and more specifically ideological response, to the major social and political struggles of the last 200 years, which has been translated into an academic professional context'. The point is, whose response and whose problems? If in Africa the response and the problems are seen as those of the white man — as a white response to the white struggle to understand and govern the black man — then this is nothing less than academic colonialism.

Poverty has been one of the problems with which South African sociologists have been struggling since the 1930s. In the English-speaking centres of Rhodes and Cape Town, and recently in Natal, the concern has been with black poverty — in the Afrikaans centres of

Stellenbosch and Pretoria, the concern was with white poverty; but whereas white poverty has been virtually eradicated, black poverty is a growing reality. The reasons for these two starkly different results are explained by the fact that, while the Afrikaner struggled with and responded to his poverty himself, the African is prohibited from doing so. He is obliged to have 'trustees' acting on his behalf, but the trustees can only see his poverty from outside. Incapable of experiencing it, they are incapable of eliminating it. They see it as problematic for white domination and end up producing a Poverty Datum Line which functions as a norm to square conscience with high profit.

Dr Verwoerd, later to become Prime Minister of South Africa, had a radically different approach. He was not content with an academic definition of poverty. His thrust as Head of the Department of Sociology at the University of Stellenbosch was unapologetically ideological and concerned with the urgent need to raise the poor Afrikaner from the Platteland to the industrial heart, and finally to the political helm of the country.

African poverty, like Afrikaner poverty, will be eliminated when African social scientists deal with it from within and, identifying it with the general black ferment, see it as the dynamic for radical change. It is precisely because of the potential power of the black social scientist that he remains in the main excluded and expelled from the Southern African field, heading research and teaching posts in exile while black universities in South Africa continue to be staffed often by incompetent whites, whether trained or semi-trained. But for how long can the white social scientist continue to be a party to a conspiracy which in the final analysis is not only directed against the black social scientist, but against disclosure of the social reality in Southern Africa and hence against the fundamental tenet of his discipline?

The social sciences are inevitably subjective; but they provide a unique and invaluable access to social reality. Social reality, however, will elude them so long as they allow themselves to be monopolised by a particular set of mental constructs and methods, and a particular class or race of academics.

If sociology is to be the science of social order and social progress, order and progress must be defined in universalistic terms, and not from the point of view of a particular power group. The traditional seers of Islam, Hinduism, Buddhism, Christianity, Judaism and other less institutionalised ethical religious systems have invented or revealed a set of common and hence universal values. Sociologists may ignore these only at the risk of adopting parochial alternatives. The warp and woof of

76 Sociology and Universal Reality

social relations are values. This is their distinguishing quality. Values do not enter the interconnections of physical phenomena. There is thus no question of amorality or neutrality in studying these interconnections. But social relations are the results of value choices, and the choices must be measured against an 'objective', that is universal, yardstick. To continue to ignore this responsibility is to conspire against the very principles on which sociology is founded.

References

Becker, Howard, and Barnes, Harry E. *Social Thought from Lore to Science* (Harren Press, Washington, DC, 1952)

Deloria, Vine, Jr *Custer Died for Your Sins* (Avon, New York, 1972)

Hyman, Herbert H. 'The Value System of Different Classes', in Reinhard Bendix and Seymour M. Lipset (eds.), *Class, Status and Power* (The Free Press, New York, 1953)

Kahl, Joseph A. 'Some Measurements of Achievement Orientation', *American Journal of Sociology* (1965), 70, no. 6, pp. 669-81

Nicolaus, Martin, 'The Professional Organization of Sociology', in Robin Blackburn (ed.) *Ideology in Social Science* (Vintage, New York, 1972)

Parsons, Talcott 'Social Systems', in *International Encyclopedia of the Social Sciences* (Macmillan, The Free Press, New York, 1968)

Shaw, Martin 'The Coming Crisis of Radical Sociology', in Robin Blackburn (ed.), *Ideology in Social Science* (Vintage, New York, 1972)

7 THE MAGICIAN AND THE MISSIONARY

Adam Kuper

I

The first missionaries in Southern Africa were faced with discomfiting intellectual responses when they expounded the Gospels. There were, to begin with, difficulties over particular dogmas. Casalis reported:

> The objections often arose from the fact that the sublime singularity of the divine doctrines completely bewildered our scholars. I remember to have had inconceivable difficulty in convincing them that I was not mistaken in my assertion that Jesus Christ had said that His apostles should sit with Him on twelve thrones. It was beyond their conception that the King of kings should carry His condescension so far as to render mere servants shares in his prerogatives. (1862, p. 113).

Such difficulties with the 'sublime singularity of the divine doctrines' might, however, have been anticipated. An equally serious problem was that a number of Africans objected not so much to the details of the Christian faith as to the fact that it was an all or nothing creed, claiming monopolistic rights in the religious field.

The Kwena Chief, Sechele, took up Christianity under the influence of Livingstone, but was for some time the sole convert in this tribe. Mackenzie later discovered that he continued 'in the performance of heathen ceremonies', but without abandoning his new faith.

> His position seemed to be one which he has not been by any means the first to occupy — that Christianity might be engrafted upon heathen customs, and that the two could go together ... The Bible, in short, did not require him to give up the customs of his ancestors, although it required him to believe in the Lord Jesus Christ. He could be an orthodox Mochuana and a good Christian at the same time. This was the position which he took up, and the tenor of many of his discourses. I have spent many of the hours of night with this clever chief in the earnest discussion of these points (Mackenzie, 1871, pp. 106-7).

Sechele's view was not uncommon, and a similar argument was urged by a Kwena medicine-man in a famous debate with Livingstone.[1] It is worth reviewing this celebrated conversation once again, in order to distinguish the three main arguments brought against Livingstone in his determination to end traditional rain-making practices. First, the rain-doctor suggested that Livingstone simply did not want rain to fall, for otherwise he would not object to demonstrably successful rain-making techniques. 'If you make rain for us', he challenged the missionary, 'I shall let it (medicine) alone'.

Missionary: I do wish rain most heartily, and I think your work tends to drive away rain and displeases God. He wishes us to feel our dependence on Him alone, and though you say you pray to him all the women in the town believe that you make the rain . . .
Rain-doctor: Well, if you wish rain and pray to God for it, why does it not come? You fail as well as we.
Missionary: We pray for it but do not make it. We leave it to his good pleasure to give or withhold it. You say you pray to him, but you believe you make it independent of him.
Rain-doctor: And so we do. We make it, and if people — witches — did not hinder us by their witchcraft you would soon see it . . . Whose rain was that which fell lately but mine? And by whom did the people eat corn for so many years? Who caught the clouds for them but me?
Missionary: The rain was given by God, and would have fallen had you let your medicines alone.
Rain-doctor: Of course, and it is so with all medicines, people get well though they use no medicines (Schapera (ed.), 1960, pp. 242-3).

This was an argument about causality, and it was argued basically on the level of assertion and counter-assertion, both protagonists nimbly evading possible tests of efficacy. At this level, Tswana and Christian doctrines were clearly seen by both parties to be in competition. But the rain-doctor tried also to persuade Livingstone that although their beliefs might appear incompatible, they could coexist as fellow-professionals. Addressing Livingstone in his role as a physician (a role which Livingstone did not attempt to distinguish from his role as a missionary), the rain-doctor said 'I use my medicines, and you employ yours; we are both doctors, and doctors are not deceivers'. Livingstone would have none of this: 'I think you deceive both them and yourself'. The rain-doctor replied: 'Well, then, there is a pair of us [meaning both are rogues]' (Livingstone, 1857, pp. 24-5).

The Magician and the Missionary

But it was the third line of argument deployed by the rain-doctor, echoing Sechele, which remained unanswered. Africans had been fated by God to a number of ills unknown to Europeans, and they had not been granted many of the gifts with which the Europeans had apparently been so liberally endowed. Yet

> God has given us one little thing, which you know nothing of. He has given us the knowledge of certain medicines by which we can make rain. *We* do not despise those things which you possess, though we are ignorant of them. We don't understand your book, yet we don't despise it. *You* ought not to despise our little knowledge though you [Livingstone] are ignorant of it.

In other words, both parties possessed a specific and relevant 'truth'; and these truths were not mutually exclusive.

Livingstone presented these arguments as representative specimens of Kwena objections to the Christian message. 'These arguments are generally known, and I never succeeded in convincing a single individual of their fallacy, though I tried to do so in every way I could think of' (ibid.). At the same time Livingstone recognised a basic kinship in the ultimate theory of divine causality which lay behind the views of both parties, and he criticised Moffat for having denied this (Schapera (ed.), 1974, pp. 100-1).

The syncretist position which may be discerned in the responses of the Kwena intellectuals to the London Missionary Society was duplicated elsewhere in Southern Africa, but — with the scandalous exception of Bishop Colenso in Zululand — even the least dismissive of the missionaries could not stomach such views. The majority were adamant that their Gospel could not coexist with African magic and religion. For some, these were practices of the Devil; for others they were mere shams and superstitions. In neither case, however, could they be countenanced by the Church.

The problem was not simply doctrinal. On the whole, the missionaries refused to tolerate a wide variety of African social practices, which they felt were un-Christian, particularly polygyny, bridewealth and initiation. A true Christian life was impossible until the social order of the African tribe was radically altered. This implied, and the early missionaries accepted the implication in many cases, that the political position of traditional religious authorities, including the chiefs, had to be challenged. Some virtually took over the leadership of the tribes themselves, as Moffat did among the Tlhaping, while others segregated the Christian factions under their leadership, creating virtually distinct Christian tribes bounded socially and often physically from heathen influence.[2] Thus the dualistic and holistic doctrinal views of the missionaries had, to varying degrees, implications for their secular ambitions. Political and social reforms had to be made not merely in order to facilitate the work of the missionary but in order to create that new anti-pagan society in which a Christian life would be possible. Although the ideological underpinnings of missionary policies have been neglected by scholars, this secular aspect of their endeavour has been comparatively well-documented. The 'missionary' factor in tribal and imperial politics has been analysed by several historians. Anthropologists have studied the secular conditions which facilitated conversion (as in Hilda Kuper's study of the differential appeal of Christianity to various segments of Swazi society) and, more commonly, described the secular consequences, such as the social segmentation caused by Christian segregation in some parts of the country (Mayer, 1961), the development of distinctive Christian family structures (Krige, 1975), the effects on traditional moral sanctions (Schapera, 1933), and so forth.

Given the historical development of Southern Africa, it is not surprising that the political dimension of the missionary endeavour, and of African Christianity, should have been given particular prominence by scholars. Thus Hilda Kuper stressed the political role of the missionaries in Swaziland. They 'accentuated differences and bolstered European domination' (1947, p. 128). Sundkler's classic study analysed the emergence of Independent African churches partly in terms of political processes in South Africa (1948, Chs. 2-4), and in the second edition of his monograph he emphasised the conservative role played by many of the separatist churches in post-War Southern African politics (1961, pp. 302-23).

Professional historians dealing with the missionaries have concentrated almost exclusively on their political roles, particularly *vis-à-vis* colonial and imperial governments.[3] For some Marxist scholars, the political functions of African Christianity explain the phenomenon entirely. Thus Mafeje concludes that Christianity (though once perhaps a 'progressive' force in Southern Africa) is really 'false consciousness', and he therefore welcomes the fact that among young men in Langa in the 1960s all Christian churches, whether orthodox or independent, were regarded as frauds, serving white interests (1975, p. 176).

Despite this interest in the secular dimension of the conversion process, the intellectual underpinnings of the missionary view have not been seriously examined. Even more fundamentally, the emphasis of (particularly) non-Christian scholarship has drawn attention away from the intellectual and spiritual reaction of Africans. Yet, as Leo Kuper wrote, commenting on a part of the problem:

> Granted that the separatist churches provide avenues of leadership and self-expression, that the motivation may not be purely religious, and that to some extent religious separatism is an alternative for political action, nevertheless the presence of a Christian idiom in these churches seems ample testimony of the significance of Christianity for Africans. To this I would also add the evidence of bitter denunciation by Africans and rejection of Christian practice, and indeed of Christianity, which is meaningful only against a background of deep religious commitment (1965, p. 192).

We must take the conversion seriously in its own terms, in its meaning both for missionaries and for Africans.

II

The missionaries began with an absolute dichotomy between Christian and pagan, and they saw the ultimate triumph of Christianity as inevitable, on doctrinal grounds and also, in some cases, for broadly 'evolutionist' reasons.[4] This dichotomy between Christian and pagan was not concurrent with the South African settler opposition between African and European, regarded as genetically determined, irrevocably distinct human types. South African whites often had a lot of trouble, for example, with the idea of the black Christian; but this was not a phenomenon which struck the missionary as problematic in any way. The missionary approach, often broadly liberal in African terms, had more in common with the views of the last generation of liberal colonial administrators, who also saw African societies tending towards the gradual but inevitable and beneficent adoption of European mores. This tension between the missionary Christian/pagan opposition and the settler white/black opposition was the source of much liberal missionary criticism of government policy in South African history.

The missionary perspective implied, particularly in the early days, that African converts must perceive Christianity much as any other Christian was expected to perceive it. The breakthrough into a more questioning approach came as a consequence of the brute fact that African Christians left the mission and orthodox churches in large numbers for new movements of doubtfully Christian identity, the 'Independent' or 'Separatist' churches. This movement provoked

Sundkler's *Bantu Prophets in South Africa,* a study which not only illuminated the whole problem but initiated a striking shift in missionary attitudes. Sundkler developed a secular thesis which explained the emergence of these churches with reference to the contradictions between missionary preaching and settler practice, and to the example of Protestant denominationalism. However, his driving interest was to discover, in these churches, 'what the African Christian, *when left to himself,* regarded as important and relevant in Christian faith and in the Christian church' (1948, p. 17; cf. Sundkler, 1976). This concern foreshadowed a new missionary receptivity to African religious ideas, a post-colonial missionary syncretism which has become increasingly significant in contemporary missionary thinking in Africa. However, it did not initiate a total break with the traditional missionary view of the place of Christianity in African religious life.

Despite the great originality of Sundkler's work, neither he nor the scholars who soon followed him rejected the fundamental missionary opposition between Christian and pagan. What they did rather was to interpose a third, intermediate, type of religion, African Christianity. Largely through Sundkler's influence, these churches came to be seen as possibly viable local adaptations of the Christian religion; as possible termini in Africa in the evolution towards Christianity. Thus a recent writer concluded that:

> The independent churches draw on both Christianity and tradition; the movement started from a Christian and not a pagan base, but it drew on African as well as western tradition. The resulting synthesis has succeeded — where the mission churches have not — in meeting the needs of many of the people of Soweto (West, 1975, p. 189).

Evolutionism has been modified; local adaptations, variant paths have been discerned; but the broad tendencies are still perceived in essentially the traditional fashion. The two poles of paganism and Christianity mark the boundaries of the historical movement, and if African Christianity is to some degree a synthesis, it stands towards the Christian pole and is analysed as a complete institutional alternative to both paganism and the missions. The old missionary vision has been modified, but the Kwena rain-doctor is still ignored, for he saw Christianity as a distinct but not necessarily incompatible cult, to be added to, but not merged with, the existing cults.

The old dichotomy is preserved even more clearly in Wilson's theory of conversion (1971). Paralleled elsewhere in African scholarship

(Horton, 1971), it nevertheless represents one of the few serious attempts to account for the phenomenon in intellectual terms, rather than with reference to political factors, or social deprivation. Briefly, the argument is that, particularly as a consequence of the changes in the scale of social life which followed colonial intervention, Africans discovered that the petty gods of the tribal societies no longer adequately reflected their effective range of social experience, and they developed a more all-embracing faith in the formerly marginal 'High God', a development hospitable to the reception of the Christian message. This argument recalls some Christian theories concerning the development of Christianity out of Judaism within the Roman Empire, but for present purposes it is sufficient to make one general comment and one objection. The general point is that this theory further enshrines the traditional view that the Christianisation of pagan Africa is an inevitable evolutionary movement from one type of religion to another, and that in consequence the persistence of certain pagan beliefs and rites should be viewed as transitional phenomena (Wilson, 1971, Chs. 2 and 3). Sundkler's work has intervened, and Independent churches rather than mission churches are seen as a possible terminus of the movement, but the same view of history is retained. This dichotomous and evolutionary perspective is precisely my target in this paper.

The particular objection is that the thesis seems to require an African perception of Christianity as a single, unified and universalistic religion. This is a real difficulty. Sundkler himself noted that 'The eight hundred Bantu Independent churches in South Africa are, as it were, the arithmetical progression of sectarian divisions in the West', and commented: 'Not only African "Separatist" Churches, but also many European missionary organisations bring to mind Coleridge's phrase: "I belong to that universal and invisible church, of which I actually am the only member" ' (1961, pp. 295-6).

Leo Kuper has quoted the Rev. Mokitimi's observation that the denominationalism of the missions 'suggested a new form of tribalism and contributed towards the ease with which secession took place and new "tribes" were formed' (1965, p. 194). It is well-known that political advantage was taken of this sectarianism by chiefs, who played one mission off against another, particularly if the missionaries were drawn from different nations. Some chiefs seem even to have taken the view that they could and should develop a national church, a Christianity which would reinforce tribal boundaries, as on the whole the Tswana chiefs seem to have done (Pauw, 1965, pp. 242-6). Now it may well be that the Africans saw through denominationalism and perceived, correctly or otherwise, that all forms of Christianity were fundamentally one; that the organisational chaos masked a deeper unity. Indeed I think there is considerable truth in this, but I do not believe that it strengthens Wilson's case. In my view many African intellectuals — like the Kwena rain-doctor — took a Hindu rather than a Christian view of religious coexistence. They believed that ultimately all religions shared a common basis, and they were inclined to incorporate traditional and universal creeds in a single philosophical framework. Against Wilson and the missionaries, then, I discern an African view which posits not an evolutionary displacement but rather a process of accommodation. But we must first try to uncover the African perception of Christianity, as a religion, without relying on the assumptions of the missionaries.

III

My interest in these problems was stimulated by fieldwork in western Botswana, among the Kgalagari. I was not far from the site of Livingstone's encounter with the rain-doctor, and, like Livingstone, I found myself in the middle of a drought, and had to watch the people trying desperately to cope with it. But there were no missionaries in this part of the Kalahari, and although Christianity had been established for generations, it was possible (in Sundkler's phrase) to see what happened when the African Christian really was 'left to himself'.

There are ten African villages in the Gantsi and Northern Kgalagadi districts of Botswana, islands of human settlement focussed on the oases of the Kalahari desert, the 'pans'. Gantsi and Kgalagadi districts cover an area of about 90,000 square miles of west and south-west Botswana, and together have a population of 32,700 (1964), of whom ten to eleven thousand live in the ten villages and some small hamlets attached to them. These African villages are in the west central part of the area, and are the only substantial human settlements in southern Gantsi and northern Kgalagadi districts. The inhabitants belong to four main tribal groups: the Kgalagari, the largest grouping, comprising over half the total; Tswana (Tlharo and Rolong), Herero, and Nama (Hottentot). Some villages have bands of Bushmen loosely dependent upon them, and some Kgalagari have Bushmen serfs.[5] The Kgalagari and Tswana are culturally and linguistically cognate, and Herero and Nama men (refugees from anti-German rebellions in South West Africa) generally speak these languages fairly well.

With the exception of the Bushmen, the people of the desert depend mainly on cattle and goats, cattle now producing a significant cash income. They also farm cereals, beans and melons which, however, are not dependable, because of the scarcity and uncertainty of the rains. They also hunt, mainly for the skins, and engage themselves, to a limited extent, as migrant labourers.

A couple of small missions in the vicinity of Gantsi village (the administrative headquarters, and the centre of a predominantly white ranching settlement) serve the 'farm Bushmen', but there are no missions in the villages of the central Kalahari. Nevertheless every village has several churches, which are run by local men engaged by various Christian movements as 'evangelists'. Some have been sent for brief periods of education to Church schools, while others are simply literate men engaged on the spot. They are paid small stipends, and sometimes serve more than one village. The first Kgalagari evangelist (from Hukuntsi, the oldest of the villages) was recruited three generations ago while on a trading visit to Kuruman, where the famous London Missionary Society (LMS) mission to the Tswana was established by Livingstone's father-in-law, Moffat. The LMS is still the strongest of the movements in the Kalahari, but there are also several churches of the African Methodist Episcopalians, an American black church with a large following in South Africa. Recently some Seventh Day Adventist churches have been set up, following a visit to the area by American missionaries who engaged local evangelists.

None of the evangelists are full-time employees, and in general they earn rather less than local minor government functionaries, such as the court scribe and the primary school teacher. Their educational attainments are not unusually high, extending to basic literacy in Tswana and English, an achievement fairly common since the establishment of primary schools in the African villages in the late 1940s. The evangelists work with no real supervision, and local teachers and court scribes often stand in for them.

In addition to these churches some local prophets had recently emerged when I first came to the Kalahari in 1963. They were Christian but at least one was non-denominational, and while they officiated at services in the same way as the evangelists, and often in the same churches, they also specialised in curing and witchclearing.

A large minority of villagers was more or less formally associated with one or other of these churches, but the committed membership was made up almost entirely of women, who comprised the bulk of the routine congregations, and staffed the church committees under the leadership of the male evangelist or a teacher, court scribe or shop assistant. The distribution of male members among the churches reflected fairly accurately the factional division within the village political system. Only some evangelists barred polygynists, who in the strict sense were in any case rather rare, and they were accepted by the African Methodist Episcopalians. The most successful of the prophets, Katchipaha, a Herero, preached in any church, though he had his own church and residential clinic in his home village. At the peak of his success, in the early 1960s, he sometimes brought entire villages together in prayer. There was no serious competition, either doctrinal or evangelical, between the various churches. They rose and fell in local importance according to the impetus given by individual evangelists and the favour of particular headmen.

The churches were thus in the hands of ordinary local people. They certainly set themselves up as guardians and critics of morality, but not from the essentially foreign perspective of mission churches. Preachers might inveigh against drink and tobacco, but their most telling attacks were on 'jealousy' (*lehuha*), a euphemism for witchcraft. Some churches banned polygynists, but not all; and the current sexual permissiveness was in general taken for granted. This set them off from mission churches; but what was their attitude to explicitly pagan beliefs and customs?

This is a difficult issue. The main Tswana and Kgalagari cults are generally listed as initiation ceremonies, rain and first-fruit ceremonies, and ancestor worship. Of these three clusters of religious activities, the place of ancestor worship is distinctly uncertain. Schapera alone states baldly that 'The dominant cult was the worship of the dead' (1953, p. 59), but his main sources are far less precise; and one can read Willoughby's (1928) study as a desperate and losing attempt to attribute Tswana religious practices to a shadowy but supposedly dominant belief in ancestral spirits. Pauw begins with Schapera's assertion, but finds little or no evidence for it, and even recounts how a 'group of men in a headman's *kgotla*' told him 'that the Tswana do not have the custom of "giving to the ancestor spirits" — it is a custom of the Southern Sotho and Nguni people' (1960, p. 25). I cannot attempt to resolve the problem here, but certainly the Kgalagari never described to me a former ancestral cult, nor can I find obvious traces of one in the literature on the Tswana.[6] We are left then with initiation ceremonies, and rain and first-fruit ceremonies.

Both these types of ceremony were attacked by missionaries among the Tswana.[7] As I shall describe later, the rain ceremonies persisted in some form, but some cults and practices were abandoned. Was this a result of Christian attack? It is at least arguable that the cults which fell into disuse were those which were most closely connected with the political position of the chief, and that they decayed as his office changed in nature under British colonial rule. Nobody among the Kgalagari suggested to me that initiation ceremonies had been discontinued as a consequence of Christianisation. Indeed, Christian influence was not even mentioned in this connection. The last ceremonies had been held in the late 1940s, at the same time as primary schools were introduced into the area, and the old men told me that they had been reluctantly persuaded to discontinue the ceremonies because they suspected that the District Commissioner was antagonistic, and because the young men were unwilling to submit to them. The local headman wanted to hold them — the age regiments were a traditional source of chiefly authority — but did not have the means to enforce his will.

A further complication is introduced by the common use of the old-fashioned dichotomy between 'religious' and 'magical' beliefs and practices. Thus Pauw contrasts the decline of 'pagan religion' among the Tlharo of the Cape with the continued strength of magic'. (1960, Ch. 2; Schapera, 1953, p. 61, 1969). Under this head comes the use of medicines, including rain medicines, the beliefs in witchcraft and sorcery, and various 'superstitions'. There is a certain utility in this distinction, to the extent that it reflects the classic opposition between religions, which involve congregations, and magic, which is viewed as a private and individual transaction (Robertson-Smith, 1889; Durkheim, 1915). In the Kalahari everyone firmly believed in the malign activities of *baloi* (witches) and in the danger of other mystical sources of attack; they feared the destructive power of the lightning bird; they told stories of the wicked spirits (*badimo*) (Brown, 1926, Ch. 12); and they patronised witch doctors, Bushmen medicine dancers, and various rain makers. Thus one great public cult, the initiation ceremonies, had vanished; the other, rain making, had been transformed; but the more private beliefs and practices persisted, apparently very little changed. However, they persisted alongside 'science', in the guise of veterinary officials and 'dispensers' (Botswana's barefoot doctors), who were equally well-patronised, often by the same people who went, also, to more traditional experts; and alongside prophets and evangelists with different claims. These different remedies persisted side by side, and without any apparent strain. Neither the believers nor, for the most part, the practitioners saw their various religious and magical techniques as being philosophically or socially incompatible. Thus it could be argued that the magical beliefs flourish still where religious cults do not, because they were less closely tied to particular political institutions, rather than because Christianity has thrust pagan religion aside while for some reason not successfully challenging magic (but cf. van Binsbergen, 1976).

Yet the magic/religion dichotomy obscures more than it illuminates. If one compares the content of the various types of magico-religious activity, deep similarities become apparent. Possession, for example, happened to women in churches, to prophets during services, to some witch doctors in seances, and to some Bushmen in curing dances. To the observer, Kgalagari or foreign, there was obviously great similarity in these occasions, and all would be explained with reference to *badimo* (spirits).

The underlying agreement between practitioners of various cults came home to me when I collected autobiographical accounts in which they explained the way in which they had found their vocations. I shall present three, the first from a Kgalagari evangelist of the LMS:

> I became a minister by the love of God. In 1924 I was a policeman in Gantsi. Then, on a journey between Olifantskloof and Gantsi, my ox-waggon broke down. I was alone, without food, water or anything. It was daytime. I was resting when I heard a voice saying I must read a particular chapter and verse in the Book of John. I was very sorry because I could not read. Then when I woke up I found a New Testament in my pocket. I took it out and opened it and saw the verse and, although I could not read, when I looked at it I heard a voice reciting it. My reading stopped there. Then I read that verse for two months until I could read a bit.

He told me that even as a boy he had been a Christian, but that this vision was the key event in his spiritual life, and that when in 1957 he became an evangelist, he dedicated himself 'by that verse'.

The Herero Prophet, Katchipaha, also told me that God had made him a prophet, by means of direct visions from heaven while asleep. Indeed, his visions were remarkably similar to those of the LMS evangelist. More interesting, perhaps, was his image of his work:

> I try to help our black people — any black people. Because we Africans have many medicines with which to kill people during the night. And there are witch doctors. I stopped that. I try to bring to them the word of God, and I give them water which I pray over. This water did them good, it healed all sorts of diseases.

The attack on witch doctors was made by evangelists also, and was based on the notion that African medicines were fundamentally ambiguous, possibly used for witchcraft as well as curing; unlike the water which only 'did good'. The third text, from a well-known Kgalagari witch doctor in Hukuntsi, is therefore particularly interesting. First he explained, like the evangelist and the prophet, that his calling came from God, and that he had been elected in a dream.

> One day I was asleep and I dreamt that I was treating a lean old woman. I cut her finger and put a medicine into the cut. When I awoke in the morning, I started work. If even your eye is sore, I can heal it. Or even your stomach.

But Katchipaha had banned African medicines, he told me, so now he cured only by cutting and sucking out harmful objects implanted by witches. I asked why the prophet had banned medicines but not incisions, and he said he did not know. A bystander explained: 'Because some of the doctors were bewitching people — some, though, were helpful'.

The fact that Katchipaha was temporarily on the ascendant, while the witch doctor was on the defensive is not, I think, significant. What is more interesting is the fact that they operated within a common cosmology of mystical forces, and, with the evangelist, accepted a common source and manner of divine appointment and legitimation. There are different cults, different specialists, but while in competition at one level they are united in a shared basic understanding of their world and the place of ritual experts within it. They are in command of distinctive skills but they are all spokesmen for the common religious views of the common man, firmly rooted in the local culture and serving the established needs of the people.

The ultimate religious unity of the community and its specialists was underlined during the drought of 1963-4. There were prayers in the LMS church. Katchipaha held a moonlight prayer meeting in the pan. Bushmen were paid to do rain dances. A witch doctor was employed to use rain magic. All these specialists were tapped by the headman on behalf of the community, and many villagers attended all the rituals. I was told that in an earlier year the prophet had held a prayer meeting at the grave of the headman's father. Similarly, individuals would run the gamut of available specialists in treating illness, with no sense of incongruity or disloyalty.

Thus the evolution of religious beliefs in the Kalahari, not obscured by the constant imposition of white views, may be seen as a clear development from the point of view outlined by the rain-doctor in his debate with Livingstone. Accommodation is the rule. Is this then a special development, due only to the absence of white missionaries? It is certainly an extreme development, for there is none of the tension which the pressure of disapproving missionaries inevitably creates. However, there is parallel evidence of syncretism in eastern Tswana rain-making, where the chief, still ultimately responsible for the rain, may countenance the use of both Christian and pagan rites in his name (Schapera, 1971, ch. 1). Indeed, when one begins to examine the literature the evidence is abundant, but it is sometimes masked by the separate description of 'pagan relics' and 'Christian practices'. We require more integrated descriptions of actual religious expression and behaviour, without the constant imposition of extraneous divisions upon that expression.

IV

My argument is that the Christian missionaries initially envisaged their task as the introduction of a total alternative to pagan belief and custom, and that they were sustained in their work by the faith that their triumph was divinely assured, and, in some cases, by the more secular hope that broader evolutionary processes were working in their favour as well. This view has dominated later scholarship, though differently formulated, and this despite the attention granted to the Independent African churches. (These are now seen as symptoms of the general political failure of the Church in South Africa to support African interests; or, more adventurously, as possibly viable African embodiments of the Christian message.) I have opposed to this broad view an African perspective which sees Christian and African religious practices and beliefs as non-competitive; much as Christians (and Africans) see the relationship between religion and science.

I have tried to support an 'African' interpretation of the reception of Christianity by describing what happened in a region where the missionaries were not on hand to enforce their boundaries between Christian and pagan. Another example may be appropriate. The Swazi King Sobhuza is generally regarded as a firm pagan, and certainly he has been a strong critic of the political and social effects of the missions. However, he has patronised Bishop Nkonyane, a Swazi Zionist church leader, and since 1938 has granted him a presence at the national *incwala* ceremony. Moreover, a new national feast has been initiated, *iGoodi*, based on Good Friday, led by Nkonyane, Sobhuza and the

Queen Mother (Sundkler, 1965, pp. 282-6). At the very least it must be granted that the Christian/pagan dichotomy is less apparent to many Africans than to many churchmen and scholars in Southern Africa. Pauw even reports that Xhosa pagans might talk of themselves as 'Wesleyan heathens' or 'Anglican heathens', while in the Northern Cape he once heard a reference to 'LMS heathens', which would have appalled Livingstone but been readily accepted by the rain-doctor (Pauw, 1965, p. 251). There are, of course, many Africans who have internalised the mission view (Kiernan, 1974, p.19),[8] but the pervasiveness of African syncretist ideologies and judgments is of great significance.

This conclusion, however tentative, cannot serve as a resting-place. One begins to perceive that the domination of the Christian perspective has had further serious consequences for the understanding of contemporary Southern African religion. First, as elsewhere in Africa, the religion of the missionaries and the orthodox African Christians has been neglected by scholars.[9] This failure may be criticised on various grounds, but perhaps the most serious consequence is that the religious institutions which are subjected to scrutiny are decontextualised. Sundkler has been criticised for the sharpness of his dichotomy between Ethiopian and Zionist churches (West, 1975, pp. 16-21), but a more serious difficulty is his implicit dichotomy between Independent and orthodox Christianity. In a recent study of African members of a Dutch Reformed Church, Schutte asked a sample of congregants whether they saw any important difference between their own and other mission churches. Seventy per cent replied that there was no difference. More to the point,

> Sixty per cent perceived superficial differences between their church and the Zionists, whereas forty per cent maintained that they were the same. Changing one's church affiliation, thus, does not pose any grave problems. Twenty-four per cent of the members had been confirmed in the Dutch Reformed Church. Fifty per cent came from other established mission churches and twenty six per cent were previously members of independent churches (Schutte, 1974, p. 114)

Beginning from what I have called the African perspective, a different sort of scholarship might have developed, dealing with the whole gamut of contemporary religious ideas and agencies within one historical but non-evolutionary framework. Hilda Kuper anticipated such an appeal, in a teasing passage whose title, 'Missionary and Magician', I have borrowed for this paper:

> Between missionary (*umfundisi*) and Swazi ritual specialist (*inyanga*) exists a common bond: though they openly condemn and criticise each other's beliefs these beliefs are rooted in an unrealised and inadmissable similarity . . . There is little to distinguish the diviner's claim to achieve his ends through inspiration from the ancestral spirits from the claim of Zionist 'prophets' to possession by the Holy Ghost (*Umoya Oyincwele*). Nor can the average Swazi appreciate the fine distinction drawn by Catholics between obsession and possession, each state being provided for in a prescribed ritual. One Roman Catholic Father actually says that he is a better 'magician' than any Swazi, and by means of a peculiar instrument divines illness, loss of property and the distribution of various metals.
>
> Many 'magicians' incorporate items of missionary teachings into their work, and add an appeal to God or Jesus to their recital of ancestral guardian spirits. One famous diviner always included a garbled Latin prayer in his preliminaries . . . (1947, p. 126).

This is the voice of the freethinker, not often heard in discussions of African religion in Southern Africa; but it is also a statement of facts which Southern African scholars have too often neglected.

As Hilda Kuper hinted, it may not be sufficient even to rest with the conclusion that Southern African black religious life must be approached as a whole, and without predetermined dichotomies and evolutionary expectations. It may be that the relationship between white and black religion is closer (though more complex) than appears at first sight. I found a hint of this in the first field study I carried out, as an undergraduate in Johannesburg, amongst witch doctors who catered for domestic servants in a wealthy white suburb. I found that in every block there was a part-time medicine-man, and that he found a regular stream of customers amongst the servants, who generally belonged to various African churches as well. I was more surprised, however, to discover that their white 'madams' often believed in their magical powers, and would quickly sack anyone they found meddling with 'black magic'.

But my final shock came when my mother begged me to abandon the study. Her servant, my former nanny, had persuaded her that I was endangering myself by coming into contact with African magic.

What are the implications of ignoring the unspoken academic dichotomy between black and white religion in Southern Africa? One might argue that the sort of analysis which has been applied to African churches would fit equally some white churches. In October 1974 the

General Synod of the Nederduitse Gereformeerde Kerk

> resolved, by an overwhelming majority, that it would regard its ties with the Netherlands Reformed Churches as broken unless the decision to support terrorism on the South African borders was rescinded not later than the first session of the next synod (*A Survey of Race Relations in South Africa*, 1974, p. 49.)

This certainly recalls Sundkler's description of the genesis of African separatist churches (1948, Ch. 2). If one's aim were the understanding of fundamental movements in South African Christianity it would, however, probably be more illuminating to study the orthodox churches which incorporate large congregations of white and black, perhaps particularly the Methodists with their integrated congregations and organisation.

At this stage my argument seems to tend toward the sociological platitude that the religious life of a society must be understood as a whole, and in relation to its total social structure. This simple rule has not been followed in Southern African studies because South Africa is a plural society; and it is therefore perceived by the ruling community as being divided into two distinct societies with distinct cultures.

Let me recapitulate. I have argued that the original missionary vision has been remarkably tenacious and pervasive. It has even determined the framework within which the study of African religious life in Southern Africa has been carried out. This is an implicitly evolutionary framework, envisaging a march from paganism to Christianity; and within this initial dichotomy, later, subtler but essentially compatible dichotomies have been incorporated, between magic and ('traditional') religion, and between Independent and orthodox Christianity. I suggested earlier that the missionary opposition between Christian and pagan did not parallel the settler opposition between European and African, and that there is a tension between their models. Nevertheless, the missionaries, and their scholarly successors, probably unconsciously, mitigated the tension by concentrating their researches on the religious life of those Africans who were not orthodox Christians; a concentration which is easily accommodated to the settler notion that it is the Africanness of blacks which is noteworthy. Thus white Christianity and also multiracial orthodox Christianity have been ignored; and, even more fundamentally, there has been no attempt to look at Southern African religious life as a whole. Just as the regime postulates the existence of separate black and white societies, so the scholars have, on the whole, concentrated on apparently distinct black religious institutions. Yet there is a strong case for arguing that Southern African society is becoming more integrated, and that one would expect the religious life to reflect this.

Leo Kuper wrote:

> As the races grow more and more interdependent in the urban and industrial economy, and as increasing contact offers greater opportunity for association, in almost the same measure, the government passes and implements laws against interracial association and enforces separation in an ever-extending range of relationships. But the paradox is only a seeming one. There is too much interdependence to sustain the threat of severance or divisive conflict. In fact, apartheid restructures the society by an elaboration of intercalary institutions and structures, which bind together, as with hoops of steel, the units-in-separation. Whether the process is likely to be a continuous and increasing binding together until the groups suddenly explode in violence, a revolution through integration, or whether this binding together may generate more gradual processes of change, I do not know (1974, p. 160).

The religious institutions of the society must reflect, in part, these apparently paradoxical processes, and may even, in turn, affect them. Protestant Christianity has provided the intellectual idiom in which generations of South Africans have reflected upon their fate, and in terms of which oppression has been justified and criticised, and individuals have found the strength to accept their suffering, or to rebel against it. It is remarkable then that so little work has been done on the development and modality of this single dominant ideology, in a society increasingly integrated and yet increasingly riven by the most profound conflicts.

Notes

This paper has been much improved as a result of the stimulating criticism of my colleague Wim van Binsbergen.

1. The debate was noted in Livingstone's Private Journals, in 1853. In his edition of the Journals, Schapera noted: 'The published version of this famous dialogue (*Missionary Travels in South Africa*, pp. 23-5) is both shorter and also differs in many details from that given above. Still another version is found on pp. 78-81 of a notebook in the Livingstone Memorial, Blantyre' (Schapera (ed.), 1960, p. 239n). I have not seen the Blantyre version, but the differences between

the two published versions are unimportant and do not seem to reflect any attempt at self-censorship. It may be that the debate was less a verbatim transcription than a recreation and dramatisation of typical arguments.

2. See R. Moffat, *Missionary Labours and Scenes in Southern Africa* (1842), and compare Dachs (1972).

3. The *locus classicus* is Macmillan (1929); Dachs (1972) is a good modern example.

4. See for example, Willoughby (1923), or indeed Mackenzie (Dachs (ed.), 1975, p. 63ff).

5. For a detailed account see A. Kuper (1970). An up-to-date bibliography can be found in the 'supplementary bibliography' published with the 1976 reprint of Schapera's *The Tswana* (1953).

6. To support his contention, Schapera cites Brown (1926, pp. 97-108); Willoughby (1928, *passim*), and Language (1941).

7. For the differential reaction of various Tswana tribes to these demands for changes in such fields as cult activity, bridewealth and the use of alcohol, see Schapera, (1970).

8. Even a Zionist church may be fiercely exclusive (Kiernan, 1974), and one must, of course, distinguish the latitudinarianism of the laity from the strict shepherding of Ministers.

9. Beidelman (1974) has recently argued strongly for the anthropological study of missions, and reviews the sadly limited work which has been done in this field in Africa (Arens, 1976). A useful, but as yet unpublished, study is Blanchet-Cohen (1976).

References

Arens, W. 'Islam and Christianity in sub-Saharan Africa: ethnographic reality or ideology?' *Cahiers d'Etudes Africaines* (1976) 59, vol, 15, 3, pp. 443-56

Beidelman, T.O. 'Social theory and the study of Christian missions', *Africa* (1974) vol. 44, 3, pp. 235-49

Binsbergen, W.M.J. van 'The dynamics of religious change in Western Zambia', *Ufahamu* (1976) vol. 16, 3, pp. 69-87

Blanchet-Cohen, T. 'French-Canadian Catholic Missionaries in Lesotho' (unpublished M Phil thesis, University of London, 1976)

Brown, J.T. *Among the Bantu Nomads* (Seeley, Service, London, 1926)

Casalis, Rev. E. *The Basutos* (James Nisbet, London, 1861)

Dachs, A.J. 'Missionary Imperialism – the case of Bechuanaland', *Journal African History* (1972), vol. 13, 4, pp. 647-58

—— (ed.) *Papers of John Mackenzie* (Witwatersrand University Press, Johannesburg, 1975)

Durkheim, E. *Elementary Forms of Religious Life* (Allen and Unwin, London, 1915)

Horrell, M., D. Horner and J. Hudson, *A Survey of Race Relations 1974* (South African Institute of Race Relations, Johannesburg, 1974)

Horton, R. 'African conversion', *Africa* (1971), vol. 41, p. 2, pp. 85-108

Kiernan, J.P. 'Where do Zionists draw the line?', *African Studies* (1974) vol. 33, p. 2

Krige, E.J. 'Traditional and Christian Lovedu family structures', in M.G. Whisson and M. West (eds.), *Religion and Social Change in Southern Africa* (David Philip, Cape Town, 1975)

Kuper, A. *Kalahari Village Politics: an African Democracy* (Cambridge University Press, London, 1970)

Kuper, H. *The Uniform of Colour* (Witwatersrand University Press, Johannesburg, 1947)
Kuper, L. *An African Bourgeoisie: Race, Class and Politics in South Africa* (Yale University Press, New Haven and London, 1965)
——, *Race, Class and Power* (Duckworth, London, 1974)
Language, F.J. 'Kapteinskap onder die Tlhaping' (unpublished Ph D thesis, University of Stellenbosch, 1941)
Livingstone, D. *Missionary Travels and Researches in South Africa* (John Murray, London, 1857)
Mackenzie, J. *Ten Years North of the Orange River* (Edmonston and Douglas, Edinburgh, 1871)
Macmillan, W.M. *Bantu, Boer and Briton* (Faber and Faber, London, 1929)
Mafeje, A. 'Religion, class and ideology in South Africa', in M. Whisson and M. West, (eds.),
Cape Town, 1975)
Mayer, P. *Townsmen or Tribesmen* (Oxford University Press, London, 1961)
Moffat, R. *Missionary Labours and Scenes in Southern Africa* (Snow, London, 1842)
Pauw, B.A. *Religion in a Tswana Chiefdom* (Oxford University Press, London, 1960)
——, 'Patterns of Christianization among the Tswana and the Xhosa speaking Peoples', in M. Fortes and G. Dieterlen (eds.), *African Systems of Thought* (Oxford University Press, London, 1965)
Robertson-Smith, W. *The Religion of the Semites* (A & C Black, London, 1889)
Schapera, I. 'Premarital pregnancy and native opinion: a note on social change', *Africa* (1933, vol. 6, pp. 59-89
——, *The Tswana* (International African Institute, London, 1953)
——, 'Christianity and the Tswana', *Journal of the Royal African Institute* (1958), vol. 88, pp. 1-9
——, 'Some aspects of Kgatla Magic', in *Ethnological and Linguistic Studies in Honour of N.J. van Warmela* (Pretoria Department of Bantu Administration and Development, Ethnological Studies no. 52, 1969)
——, *Tribal Innovators: Tswana Chiefs and Social Change 1795-1940* (Athlone Press, London, 1970)
——, *Rainmaking Rites of Tswana Tribes* (Afrika Studie Centrum, Leiden, 1971)
——, (ed.) *Livingstone's Private Journals: 1851-1853* (Chatto and Windus, London, 1960)
——, (ed.) *David Livingstone's South African Papers 1849-1853* van Riebeeck Society, Cape Town, 1974)
Schutte, A.G. 'Dual religious orientation in an urban African church', *African Studies* (1974), vol. 33, p. 2
Sundkler, B. *Bantu Prophets in South Africa* (Oxford University Press, London, 1948) (second revised edition, 1961)
——, 'Chief and prophet in Zululand and Swaziland' in M. Fortes and G. Dieterlen (eds.), *African Systems of Thought* (Oxford University Press, London, 1965)
——, *Zulu Lion* (Oxford University Press, London, 1976)
West, M. *Bishops and Prophets in a Black City* (David Philip, Cape Town, 1975)
Willoughby, W.C. *Race Problems in the New Africa* (Oxford University Press, London, 1923)
——, *The Soul of the Bantu* (Doubleday, Doran, New York, 1928)
Wilson, M. *Religion and the Transformation of Society* (Cambridge University Press, Cambridge, 1971)

8 THE AFRICAN DOCTOR: HIS ROLE IN THE COMMUNITY

Hilstan L. Watts

The professional opportunities for Africans in South Africa are still relatively few and far between, although they are gradually increasing. The 1936 through to 1970 population censuses enumerated occupations for all the various racial groups in the country. Table 1 below is the result of a regrouping, by the author, of occupations on a socioeconomic basis.

This table shows the slowly increasing percentage of Africans in upper white collar jobs. Even so, the bulk of the African population is still made up of lower blue collar workers. By 1970 still only 0.8 per cent of the Africans were in professional/higher administrative posts, compared with 8.2 per cent, or a ten times greater proportion, amongst whites. It is the upper white collar group of professional and managerial personnel which provides most or all of the leadership in modern or modernising communities. Only 1 per cent of the economically active African workers are in this category. This means that, relatively speaking, greater demands for leadership roles are placed on the African upper white collar group than is the case with the whites, where the same leadership roles can be spread over far more incumbents.

In the professional group, the main opportunities for Africans lie in the fields of law, medicine, and especially teaching. This paper concentrates on the African doctors, and presents some results of an as yet unpublished study of certain black medical students and graduates including of course Africans. (Watts, 1975, 1976[1]). The highest prestige and possibly the greatest financial rewards are in medicine. For instance, in a study amongst a selected group of Africans in Pretoria, Schmidt (1973, pp. 2, 5) found that the medical doctor had the greatest occupational prestige of various Africans, using the National Opinion Research Centre (NORC) rating scale. Therefore it is not surprising to find in a sample survey of medical students at the University of Natal that 42 per cent of the African students mentioned financial security and/or status as a reason for choosing medicine as a career (Watts, 1975, p. 8). A total of 10 per cent of the African students mentioned the fact that there were very few other alternative careers open for blacks, and this was the reason why they chose medicine as a career.

Table I: The Changing Occupational Roles of the South African Population — Percentage Distribution of Economically Active Population at Various Censuses

Occupational Category	Whites				Coloureds				Asians				Africans			
	1936	1946	1960	1970	1936	1946	1960	1970	1936	1946	1960	1970	1936	1946	1960	1970
1. Managerial & Independent Commercial	6.0	6.8	7.0	9.3	0.4	0.6	0.5	0.4	10.2	11.6	9.4	5.9	0.1	0.1	0.2	0.2
2. Professional & Higher Administrative	6.0	6.2	5.7	8.2	1.0	1.5	2.0	2.5	1.5	2.1	3.6	4.2	0.4	0.4	0.7	0.8
3. Subordinate Clerical, Commercial & Administrative workers, minor professions & subordinate technical (non-manual)	21.5	25.7	38.1	39.3	0.9	1.4	4.4	9.3	11.4	12.3	22.8	29.8	0.2	0.4	1.9	3.8
4. Independent & Managerial Agricultural Workers	22.9	17.0	9.0	5.4	2.8	2.2	1.8	0.4	10.9	9.5	9.4	1.1	0.0	0.0	0.0	—
5. Skilled Manual	16.1	16.7	15.4	15.7	8.1	8.9	10.9	12.5	8.0	9.3	11.2	9.3	0.3	0.4	0.3	4.9
6. Supervisory Manual or Manual work with some responsibility	5.2	7.2	4.9	9.2	1.5	3.0	3.1	7.6	2.4	3.9	5.6	7.4	0.4	0.7	1.9	5.3
7. Semi-skilled Manual	11.0	11.4	9.6	9.5	8.3	9.7	8.6	16.5	13.3	18.2	9.7	26.8	1.1	1.2	2.1	26.6
8. Unskilled Manual	10.5	8.3	10.2	0.7	75.6	70.8	68.9	43.0	39.7	27.8	28.3	7.7	97.0	96.2	92.9	52.8
9. Other occupations	0.8	0.8	—	2.8	1.3	1.9	—	7.8	2.72	5.3	—	7.9	0.6	0.5	—	5.7
Total Percentage	100.0	100.1	99.9	100.1	99.9	100.0	100.2	100.0	100.1	100.0	100.0	100.1	100.1	99.9	100.0	100.1
Total Number of Economically Active Workers	736,025	874,867	1,119,643	1,508,902	279,404	334,772	493,946	716,252	64,875	74,383	107,037	182,303	3,057,516	3,751,377	4,617,028	5,701,950

Sources: Union of South Africa (1942a, 1942b, 1954); Republic of South Africa (1962, 1963, 1976)
Notes: The Coloureds are white/black mixtures, Asians are almost all originally from India/Pakistan

The African Doctor

Thus just over half of the sample of African medical students gave one or more of these reasons as a basis for choosing medicine as a career. There are a small number of African medical students at the predominantly white universities of Cape Town and the Witwatersrand, but nearly all the African medical practitioners today are being trained at the University of Natal, which has the only Medical School for blacks in the country. (With effect from 1978 the University of South Africa in Pretoria will open a Medical School purely for Africans.)

At the time of the 1970 population census in the Republic, South Africa had only 175 African medical practitioners, of whom 146 were male. All but 15 of these were located in the urban areas of South Africa (Republic of South Africa, Department of Statistics, 1976, p. 231). This was out of a total of 8,757 medical practitioners reported by the census (ibid., p. 2). There were 2,706,013 economically active Africans in urban areas, and 2,995,937 in the rural areas, or a grand total of 5,701,950 African workers (ibid., p. 263).

Fieldwork impressions gained by the author and colleagues leave little doubt that the doctor in the African community is looked up to as a leader or a potential leader. In fact, some of the doctors we interviewed complained about the very high expectations which ordinary Africans had of them, and felt they could ill afford the time in a busy professional life which community roles demand. To start with, in many cases doctors emerge from training with a fairly strong altruistic motivation. For instance, amongst the medical students we interviewed, 22 per cent stated that medicine offers the opportunity of service to humanity or to their people, while 18 per cent said that the country needed more doctors. This altruism, plus the expectations of the community, tend to push the doctors into positions of prominence in the community. To what extent are the doctors acting as important community leaders? This question cannot be answered fully without fairly detailed fieldwork, but it is possible to get a brief indication from the survey done on graduates of the Medical School at the University of Natal (Watts, 1976).

Generations of medical students at the University of Natal have been somewhat 'radical' (in the South African sense of the term). This was evident long before black consciousness and black power became important movements on black campuses in the country. From teaching the students themselves today, it is evident that they are politically conscious, and highly critical of the *status quo*. They have played an active role in SASO (the union of black students which is black consciousness oriented). The currently banned persons named under the

Suppression of Communism Act no. 44 of 1950 (now renamed the Internal Security Act) have included former medical students from Durban, such as Bennie Khoapa, N. Pityana, and the late Steve Biko.

Over the past decades doctors have been important leaders of Africans. For example in the days before the African National Congress was banned, Dr A.B. Xuma and Dr James Moroka were two Presidents. Doctors together with lawyers were active leaders in the ANC. However, Kuper has commented that 'the African doctor, of all professionals, is probably in the best position to avoid political involvement' (Kuper, 1965, pp. 124-5, 234-5). It is notable that of the 101 banned persons listed in the Government Gazettes for 1975 and 1976, not one was a registered medical practitioner.

Today there is little that the African doctor can do directly about social and political discrimination, without risking being detained as a political suspect, and possibly jeopardising his or her career. However, it is in order for Africans, including doctors, to operate under the aegis of separate development, as this provides a legitimation, and allows them a political platform, provided they do not go too far in the eyes of the Security Branch of the South African Police. In the Greater Durban area Dr Frank Mdlalose, a general practitioner, is very prominent in the local politics of Kwa Mashu (a very large African township). Likewise another graduate of the University of Natal, Dr Baldwin Ngubane, is a notable member of 'Inkatha Yen-Kululeko Yesizwe Ka Zulu' – the National Cultural Liberation Movement of the Zulus' started by Chief Gatsha Buthelezi. Several doctors are prominent in other forms of the black consciousness movement in South Africa. In Soweto (Johannesburg) the Chairman of the Black Unity Front (set up by Chief Buthelezi and some other homeland leaders) is Dr Hugo Nyembezi.

The main source of information for this paper on the roles of African doctors in community activities is a sample survey undertaken by the Centre for Applied Social Sciences (formerly the Institute for Social Research) at the University of Natal (Watts, 1976). Unfortunately the fieldwork interviews sometimes show evidence of inadequate probing in this area, which was not a major concern of the survey, so the results understate the actual position. As part of this study, a sample of 32 African doctors were interviewed, mainly in South Africa and Rhodesia, but also overseas. One tenth stated they had left South Africa for political reasons, including in some cases political pressure. Questionnaires were mailed to those in the sample who could not be contacted for interviewing. A similar proportion of the replies were from doctors who had left the country on political grounds.

In examining the community involvement of African doctors, it must be remembered they carry a very heavy case load. Doctors in private practice saw an average of 53 patients per day, while the average estimated case load of doctors working in hospitals was 48 patients per day. The mean estimate for the number of operations was seven to eight daily. It appears from these figures that doctors do not have much time for non-medical commitments, and many of the doctors complained about their workload. Twenty out of the 32 doctors belonged to one or more organisations. Table II shows the type of organisations involved.

Table II: Type of Organisations to which a Sample of 20 African Doctors Belonged, 1971

Type of Organisation	no. of Doctors
Professional (Local, Regional, National)	15
Sports	12
Welfare, including health	6
Cultural	5
Religious (other than church worship)	3
Educational	2
Recreational	2
Political	1
Agricultural	1

Note: The figures are *not* mutually exclusive. Twelve out of 32 doctors in the sample did not belong to any organisations/associations, etc.

As is to be expected, the greatest proportion of doctors who were members of one or more organisations belonged to a professional medical body or bodies. This was followed in order of frequency by sports clubs (12 members), and welfare/health societies (six members). Cultural organisations of various kinds were supported by five doctors. One of these associations was 'The Association for the Educational and Cultural Advancement of the African', which appears to be similar to 'Inkatha'. Other bodies were each supported by three or less African doctors from the sample. The one doctor who is shown as supporting a political organisation in fact belonged to two of this nature. Table III shows the *number* of associations, organisations, etc., to which each of the doctors belonged. A total of 14 of the cases, or two-fifths of the doctors, belonged to three or more associations. This indicates a high degree of community involvement. The extent of this is stressed by the fact that 11 of the 32 African doctors interviewed were officer bearers in one or more associations. In fact five were office bearers in two or

102 *The African Doctor*

Table III: Number of Associations Belonged to by a Sample of African Doctors, 1971

no. of Associations belonged to	no. of Doctors	no. of Doctors *excluding* Membership of Medical Association(s)
No Associations	12	12
No Associations excluding Medical Associations	NA	3
One	4	2
Two	2	7
Three	7	4
Four	2	4
Five	4	—
Six	—	—
Seven	1	—
Total	32	32

Note: NA means 'Not Applicable'.

more associations. The offices held ranged from Chairman to that of general committee member. Table IV gives further details of the number of offices held by the doctors.

Table IV: Number of Offices Held by a Sample of African Doctors, 1971

no. of Offices held at time of survey	no. of Doctors	no. of Doctors *excluding* Medical Association(s)
None — does not belong to any association	12	12
None — belongs to one or more associations	9	9
One	6	6
Two	4	5
Three	1	—
Total	32	32

If we exclude membership of various national/regional/local medical associations, then 20 doctors, or three-fifths, belonged to one or more other bodies (Table III). This stresses the extent to which African doctors belong to community organisations of various kinds. Eleven of the doctors, or about one-third, were office bearers in one or more

The African Doctor

bodies *excluding* medical associations (Table IV).

The survey data do not provide an indication of the nature of the contributions which the doctors made to the various organisations involved, nor do they give a picture of the importance of these bodies in African life (in nearly all cases urban township life was involved). Thus, regrettably, we do not know directly what impact the doctors have on urban African thought — attitudes, goals and aspirations — but it is thought likely that they constitute an important reference group for the urban African working class.

The doctors were not, on the whole, church-goers. Twenty-nine out of the 32 described themselves as Christians, with two stating that they were atheists, and one that he was an agnostic. Eighteen out of the 29 Christians, or three-fifths, had not been to church at all during the past month before the interview. Three had been to church once during the preceding month, five twice, one three times, and only two had been weekly.

The study was not specifically directed at finding out the social and political attitudes and aspirations of the doctors. Nonetheless there were signs that at least some of the doctors felt a sense of discrimination and injustice, and sometimes also bitterness, at the white oligarchic structure of South African society. For example, the average score given to white doctors by the African doctors suggested they were at least to some extent prejudiced (Watts, 1976, pp. 27-9). This was the only negative characteristic of white doctors in terms of mean scores on a semantic-differential type test. The mean scores awarded to the hospital where each doctor had trained also showed awareness of a certain amount of prejudice involved (Watts, 1976, p. 21). Administative staff seemed more involved in this than doctors. The most frequently mentioned frustration was discriminatory pay in the hospital service, with Africans being the poorest paid of doctors.

Incomplete sentences were used in addition to semantic-differential type tests. Over a quarter completed a sentence beginning 'I hate' with a phrase involving discrimination. Almost half wrote sentences seeing whites as favoured, and as discriminating against blacks. The words 'I hope' had one-eighth writing that they hoped for freedom and political justice, and opportunities for black advancement. One-sixth responded to 'I wish I could' with wording of the type 'I wish I could have fairness and an end to inequality and discrimination'. Again one-eighth wrote 'I feel helpless ... when I think of racial discrimination and injustice'. Finally, one third followed the word 'Down' with phrases such as 'Down with discrimination, prejudice and injustice'; or 'down-trodden because of my colour is most humiliating with all forms of prejudice'. When it is borne in mind that the incomplete sentences were completed with any ideas which immediately came to mind, it is clear that the injustices and discrimination in South African society were uppermost in the minds of many of the doctors interviewed.

To sum up, it is clear that, despite heavy professional commitments, African doctors in many cases play an active role in the community. As an educational elite, they provide some of the community leadership, and enjoy great prestige. As a modernised group within urban African society they provide a reference group for the bulk of the African population, which consists of lower blue collar workers. While sensitive to discrimination and injustice, most appear to keep a low profile politically, but this could well change if and when they can be more active without jeopardising their careers.

Notes

1. The study of students, staff and graduates of the Medical School of the University of Natal was undertaken over a period of several years by the Centre for Applied Social Sciences at the University of Natal. The samples covered not only Africans, but Indians and Coloureds. Only some of the data for Africans are reported on here. The study was financed by the Human Sciences Research Council. The views expressed are those of the author only. Details of sampling schemes and research designs are given in Watts (1975 and 1976).

References

Brandel-Syrier, M. *Reeftown Elite: A Study of Social Mobility in a Modern African Community on the Reef* (Routledge and Kegan Paul, London, 1971)

Kuper, L. *An African Bourgeoisie: Race, Class and Politics in South Africa* (Yale University Press, New Haven, 1965)

Pauw, B.A. *The Second Generation: A Study of the Family among Urbanized Bantu in East London* (Oxford University Press, Cape Town, (Second edition), 1973)

Republic of South Africa, Bureau of Census and Statistics, *Population Census, 1960: Sample Tabulation No. 3 — Major Occupational Groups: Whites, Coloureds and Asiatics* (Government Printer, Pretoria, 1962), pp. 4-5, 28-9, and 46-7

——, Bureau of Census and Statistics, *Population Census, 1960: Sample Tabulation No. 5 — Industry Divisions, Age Groups, Major Occupational Groups: Bantu* (Government Printer, Pretoria, 1963), pp. 50-5

——, Department of Statistics, *Population Census 1970: Occupations (Age, Level of Education, Marital Status, Citizenship, Birthplace, National Unit)* (Government Printer, Pretoria, 1976), Report no. 02-05-11

Schmidt, J.J. *Beroepsprestige Onder die Bantoe in 'n Stedelike Gemeenskap* (Human Sciences Research Council, Pretoria, 1973), Research finding S-N-36

Union of South Africa, *Sixth Census of the Population of the Union of South Africa, enumerated 5th May 1936: Vol. 7, Occupations and Industries of the European, Asiatic and Coloured Population* (U.G. 11/1942 Government Printer, Pretoria, 1942a,) pp. 2-19, 64-75, 92-105

——, *Vol. 9, Natives (Bantu) and Other Non-European Races* (U.G. 12/1942 Government Printer, Pretoria, 1942b), pp. 71-7

——, *Population Census, 7th May, 1946: Vol. 5: Occupation and Industries of the European, Asiatic, Coloured and Native Population* (Government Printer, Pretoria, 1954), pp. 2-19, 88-106, 138-51, 180-93

Watts. H.L. 'Black Doctors: An Investigation into Aspects of the Training and Career of Students and Graduates from the Medical School of the University of Natal' (Institute for Social Research, University of Natal, Durban, unpublished report. 'Part I: The Student' 1975; 'Part II: The Graduates', 1976)

9 THE POLITICAL IMPLICATIONS OF A SPLIT LABOUR MARKET ANALYSIS OF SOUTH AFRICAN RACE RELATIONS

Edna Bonacich

The theme of this volume is the role of intellectuals in an oppressive society, a thorny problem indeed. In the field of sociology many of us have been raised on the principle of 'value free' science. The ideal is seen to be the independent thinker relentlessly pursuing his/her own interests, no matter how obscure or socially irrelevant, in the belief that only under such conditons can 'truth' emerge. Truth is, of course, a social good. Thus the selfish pursuit of knowledge by the social scientist ultimately redounds to the collective benefit.

The parallel to *laissez faire* economics in this model is obvious. And just as many have raised questions about the effectiveness, for achieving social goals, of the selfish pursuit of economic interests, so I would question the application of *laissez faire* principles to the intellectual sphere. It seems highly unlikely that an 'invisible hand' will give our intellectual endeavours a social purpose unless we put one there.

Leo Kuper's work exemplifies the conscious effort of a sociologist to keep the social and political questions alive. Much of his writing (1957, 1974; Kuper and Smith, 1969) focuses upon the dual themes of the evil and inhumanity of a racist social order, and the problem of changing such an order without initiating even greater evil and inhumanity in the process. One of the most prominent themes in his work is the achievement of significant social change by non-violent means. His is not a body of writings which only pursues abstract truth for its own sake, but represents a socially responsible search for solutions to human problems.

I have spent most of my rather brief academic career working on a theory of race and ethnic relations called the 'split labour market' (Bonacich, 1972, 1976). The purpose has been to develop a materialist understanding of the race question, with an emphasis on causes rather than solutions. Indeed I have shied away from dealing with political implications, knowing in the back of my mind that the theory leads to pessimistic conclusions. In honour of Leo Kuper, however, I shall in this short essay attempt to face some of the political implications of split labour market theory.

Split Labour Market Analysis

This volume deals with the role of the intellectual in South Africa in particular. I have recently completed a draft of a split labour analysis of that country (Bonacich, 1977), and shall base my discussion on the particulars of that society. The remainder of the essay is divided into two sections: first, a brief review of South African race relations as seen from a split labour market perspective, and second, a discussion of the political implications of the analysis.

South Africa: A Split Labour Market Interpretation[1]

In split labour market theory, the key to understanding the race question is found in discrepancies in the price of labour. The root of such discrepancies lies, not in a decision by the capitalist class to pay different groups of workers different wages in order to divide the working class, but in the historical circumstances of the workers themselves. In South Africa, from the start African (and to a lesser extent, Indian and Coloured) labour was considerably cheaper to employ than white labour. This was (and still is) true regardless of the particular job or level of skill required. If an employer in South Africa is faced with two potential employees of equivalent ability and training, one of whom is white and the other black, the former would cost him as much as fourteen times more to employ.

How did such a division come into being? While it has been elaborated upon by the class struggle which develops from split labour markets, its source predates this struggle. Briefly (and at the risk of oversimplying), African labour was cheap because the level of African economic development at the time of European conquest did not demand a 'high standard of living'. While European capital wanted African labour, and tried to coerce as well as induce the indigenous population to enter the capitalistic labour market on a full-time basis, Africans resisted. Many would migrate for a short period of time to earn a target amount of money, returning thereafter to the village community. This pattern, which frustrated capital (and led them to import more 'steady' Asians), greatly weakened African bargaining power in the labour market. For one thing, it is extremely difficult to form labour organisations among a continually changing and short-term population. For another, it is difficult for migrant workers to acquire skills with which to bargain, while employers have little incentive to provide training. There are other factors which weakened the position of Africans as workers, but the migrant labour system (initiated by an African tie to the pre-capitalist sector) is among the most important.

In contrast, white workers in South Africa were either imported skilled craftsmen, who came with trade union experience, or rural-based settlers (Boers) who were gradually pushed off the land with, by and large, no chance to return. As more stable participants in the capitalist sector, they were able gradually to organise and set minimum wages, work conditions, and living arrangements below which they were unwilling to sink.

The price discrepancy between the two groups of workers set in motion a pressure toward displacement of white labour with cheaper African labour. After all, if an employer could get the same work (or even less efficient work) for one-tenth to one-fifteenth the price, he had little reason to stick with white labour. The process or threat of displacement of white by cheaper black labour has been a dominant feature of South African history from the inception of white settlement. Even in the early Cape the question was raised as to whether the Dutch East India Company should utilise 'free white' or black slave labour, deciding in favour of the much cheaper latter option.

The displacement issue reached a peak between the end of the nineteenth century and the Great Depression, with the development of the 'poor white' problem. About ten per cent of the white population, and one-third of the Afrikaans-speaking segment, became pauperised. Employers would not hire them when cheaper African labour was readily available, and they flocked to the towns and cities, ready to support a political solution to their problem.

The tendency toward displacement was not confined to the ranks of unskilled labour. At all levels of the society there was a strain in this direction. If an employer could replace high priced white skilled workers by training less costly Africans, or by breaking down the skills into simpler segments and substituting semi-skilled black labour for a fraction of the cost, he would naturally do so. Even today there is ample evidence of this tendency as capital makes occasional forays on the colour bar and similar institutions.

The price discrepancy and consequent pressure to displacement complicated the class struggle between white labour and capital. Whenever white labour tried to improve its conditions the threat of replacement with cheap African labour loomed large in the background. The real enemy of the white working class was not African labour, but capital. Because of the weak position of the African working class, they were virtually under the control of the capitalist class, vulnerable to super-exploitation. They were seen by white labour as a tool with which capital could undermine white labour if the latter made any demands.

Split labour market theory suggests that there are a variety of ways

Split Labour Market Analysis

in which 'high priced' labour can react to the threat of displacement by cheap labour. One common reaction is exclusion, i.e., an effort to prevent cheap labour from moving into the labour market or being brought in by capital. The 'white Australia' policy, California's efforts to keep out Asian immigrants up to 1924, and current US efforts to control illegal immigration from Mexico, all stem from labour's concern over being undermined. A second strategy is to establish 'caste systems' in which there is strict job segregation, with high priced labour occupying one set of jobs at one level of pay, and cheap labour occupying another at a different pay-level. A colour bar protects high priced (white) labour from displacement in the jobs (and accompanying wages and work conditions) to which it lays claim.

A third method used by white labour to deal with the split labour market problem is to try to equalise the price of labour through legislation. Such enactments as minimum wage and maximum hour laws, or laws protecting the right to independent labour organisations, fall under this rubric. Welfare legislation, including unemployment insurance, social security, and so on, all act as supports for higher priced labour by providing cheap labour with an alternative other than undercutting the higher wage level.

Radicalism, or the active joining together of the divided elements of the workforce into a coalition against capital, is a fourth alternative. Using such a strategy, high priced labour would help to organise labour unions among cheap labour groups, and recruit them to join existing unions.

All four of these strategies are evident in South African history. White labour has tried to exclude Africans from the labour market by restricting their movement into the cities. It has set up colour bars to protect itself against displacement in particular occupations. It has fought for, and established, a standard wage in certain occupations. And it has tried to organise African workers. Not all these strategies have been followed by the same segments of the white working class nor have they been pursued with equal energy. Generally speaking, the more reactionary strategies, exclusion and caste, have emerged as the dominant mode of dealing with the split labour market in South Africa. There are a number of reasons for this, including the size of the African 'cheap labour' group, the fact that the problem was internal, the power of capital in limiting white labour's access to African workers (as in mining compounds), the extent of the initial discrepancy in standard of living, and so on. These features made the radical solution extremely difficult and pushed white labour into a narrowly self-protectionist

110 Split Labour Market Analysis

stance.

Let me emphasise that the race issue was essentially a product of class struggle between capital and white labour. Capital wanted full access to cheap African labour in order to increase profits without concern for the possibility that white labour might be displaced. Indeed, in many cases capital could use African labour as a means of keeping white labour in line. White labour, on the other hand, wanted to restrict capital's access to a tool which was so detrimental to their own wellbeing. Africans were not a direct party to this struggle much of the time. They were innocent bystanders whose fate was being determined by the other two classes.

The Rand Revolt of 1922 epitomises this struggle. Mine owners wanted to break down the colour bar, permitting Africans to do work previously done by white miners, for a fraction of the cost. White workers resisted, seeing themselves as engaged in a progressive class struggle against the abuses of the capitalist class. An oft-quoted slogan of the times, 'Workers of the world unite and fight for a white South Africa', shows the link between the race question and class struggle. The concept 'white South Africa' is similar to the concept 'white Australia' and refers, I believe, not so much to a concern over race *per se*, as to a concern over labour standards. Black labour equalled semi-slavery. A 'white' South Africa referred to a society of 'free men' who could live decently. If capital could freely make use of semi-enslaved African labour, South Africa would be unfit for 'white' habitation.

It is my contention that the Nationalist government is, in large measure, a 'white labour' regime. While not representing all segments of the white proletariat, it does speak for the majority, especially for workers at the lower end of the economic spectrum who are most directly threatened with displacement. Afrikaners tend to be among the poorer white South Africans, and the Nationalists clearly have strong support from this element.

Apartheid is an effort to solve white labour's problem by reconstructing African 'homelands' and gradually removing the urban African population to them. The goal of apartheid is exclusion. While Africans remain in the 'white' economy, the resolution to the split labour market problem is 'caste', job reservation, or strict segregation of job categories (supported by segregation in all forms of social life). But this is seen as a temporary expedient, not a desirable end-state. The Nationalists do not want a permanently hierarchical society based on black labour, with themselves in a position of a labour aristocracy. Rather, they want complete economic segregation with the white sector based entirely on high priced labour coupled with advanced technology.

The capitalist class opposes apartheid and job reservation to the extent that they keep an expensive white labour force entrenched in certain key positions and limit access to the abundant cheap labour resource of the country. Capital's goal is not an egalitarian society; it would like to be able to atomise all workers, irrespective of colour, so that the price of every worker is driven down by competition. In this sense, capital is 'colour blind'. They would hire the cheapest worker regardless of skin colour. They often appear to come out on the side of African advancement, opposing efforts to push Africans out of the urban economy, and seeking to break down the colour bar. Thus, ironically, capital often seems to promote a 'liberal' race policy, while white labour is reactionary on the race question.

In sum, I interpret South African race policy as a product of the class struggle between white labour and capital over the latter's freedom to exploit African cheap labour. Since 1948 white labour has controlled the South African state, and while the capitalist class (international as well as local) has remained strong enough to keep the threat of displacement alive, and would react fiercely if the Nationalists threatened to take over the whole economy, nevertheless white labour has been able to maintain a precarious niche for itself.

Needless to say, this brief sketch does some violence both to the details of South African history, including intra-class divisions, and to the finer nuances of split labour market theory. I have presented only the bare bones.

Political Implications

That I am not a politician will be readily apparent to the reader. Thus it is with some hesitancy that I present these rather primitive (perhaps naive) thoughts on the political implications of my model. I see this exercise as a tentative first step in an effort that ought to be tied to practical political action (as it is in the work of Leo Kuper), and cannot realistically be developed from the armchair. Nevertheless, let us plunge ahead.

Split labour market theory suggests that there is a (limited) coincidence of interests between the capitalist class and the African population, in opposition to the white working class. Both favour a 'liberalisation' of job reservation and a loosening of restrictions on African participation in the capitalist sector. While the Africans would push for much greater and quicker advances than capital is willing to support, still in the short run these two classes have a basis for joint action.

This 'paternalistic coalition', as I have called it elsewhere, is typical of split labour markets. Capital usually supports the immigration of cheap labour groups while organised labour opposes it. Capital is thus 'pro-immigrant', i.e. on the liberal side of this issue. For example, in the US it is local labour which hopes to clamp down on illegal immigration from Mexico, while capital (which can make good use of such immigrants) promotes it. (We might note that, as in South Africa, US labour sees the 'enemy' on this issue as capital, as demonstrated by efforts to hold employers culpable for hiring illegal aliens.) Similarly in the more complex world split labour market of cheap labour versus high priced labour countries, it is US labour, and the labour of other high priced labour countries, which wants to establish high tariffs and prohibit the runaway shop, while capital can (and does) claim that these measures hurt the developing countries.

The dilemma for the intellectual is that, in supporting the claims of oppressed (cheap labour) minorities, he/she is also supporting, to some extent, the interests of the capitalist class, against the interests of the white working class. Many liberal intellectuals have chosen to do just this. For example, in the dispute over Chinese immigration to California, most intellectuals supported immigration. Generally the intellectual community tends to be pro-minority and pro-immigration, which means they are often anti-white labour. I need not enumerate the many instances in which this class gets less than sympathetic treatment.

One way out of the dilemma of supporting a pro-capitalist and anti-labour position is to deny that the split labour market exists. Many radical scholars thus argue that there is no threat of displacement and that capital has duped white (or other high priced) labour into believing there is such a threat, thereby deflecting the class struggle away from capital and onto oppressed minorities. By viewing it this way, white labour is absolved (to a degree) of its racism, and capital clearly becomes the villain. One can then comfortably support the demands of oppressed minorities without at the same time having to take a stand which may be interpreted as anti-labour.

Alas this sleight of hand will not work, in my view. The reality of the displacement threat cannot be swept under the rug. Consequently the reactionary position of white labour cannot be dismissed as 'false consciousness' or the product of capitalist propaganda. There is a genuine material interest at stake here, and unless we face up to it, we will never be able to solve it.

The argument that white working-class racism is a product of capitalist propaganda suggests that the solution lies in counter propa-

Split Labour Market Analysis

ganda and education, that we can somehow persuade white (and other high priced) workers that their interests are not harmed by the presence of illegal aliens, the importing of cheap products from low wage countries, or, in the South African case, the use of Africans in jobs held by whites. The belief that such persuasion is possible is, in my view, a pipe dream. To the worker, the immediate realities speak in the opposite direction. The widespread racism and protectionism of the white working class throughout the world suggest that this problem is not easily amenable to simple persuasion.

Thus one political implication of split labour market theory, devastating to classic Marxist theory, is that, far from being the vanguard of socialist revolution, the white working class, at least in colonial settings or in settings such as Britain with its Commonwealth immigrants, which are the product of colonialism, is probably the greatest obstacle to revolution. There can be no doubt that this is true in South Africa, and it may be that the dynamics of split labour markets help to explain the failure of socialist revolution in most of the advanced capitalist societies.

Given this reality, what is to be done? The ideal resolution of the South African question (in my opinion) would be the unification of the working class, regardless of race, against international capitalism. How to achieve this is the central political problem of South Africa.

There are those who believe it is impossible, that the white working class is so corrupted as to be beyond redemption. The only solution is an African liberation movement which gives up on the white working class and 'goes it alone'. This may indeed be the only viable option, yet we should note that it is fraught with problems. For one thing, there are various difficulties within the African situation (such as the continuation of migrant labour, desperate poverty, an endless supply of cheap labour from other African countries, and so on) which make a full-fledged liberation movement difficult to attain. In addition, the problem facing an African liberation movement in South Africa is greater than for most colonial territories. They must fight not only the capitalist class, but also the large white working class, for that class is not only unwilling to engage in a joint alliance against capital, it is a positive enemy to African advance. An African liberation movement in South Africa must face two antagonists instead of one: capital and white labour. While this may be the only route available, it is bound to be extraordinarily difficult and bloody. And in the end it could fail.

Another approach is for the African people to follow the line of least resistance, i.e. join with the capitalist class to oust the white working class. Capital would support African advancement to a point. Once this goal is achieved, the problem of socialist revolution could be dealt with. In other words, the first stage is for Africans to become fully absorbed into the capitalist sector, breaking down the remaining ties to pre-capitalist economies. This could only be achieved over the opposition of white labour, but with the collaboration of capital which supports it anyway. A fully proletarianised African population could then set up the organisational basis for complete takeover. Such an approach gives up on the possibility of working class unity, and does not 'resolve' the problem so much as shift it to another locale by the ousting of one of the contenders.

My theory leads me to the position that the white working class in South Africa is not entirely corrupted even though it may appear that way on the surface. Certainly they have played a leading role in the suppression of the Africans, but not, I believe, for narrowly racist reasons. The fundamental issue for them is not that South Africa must be racially white, even though their rhetoric so asserts. If this were the case, there would be no possibility for a resolution. The real issue is cheap labour. And the white working class is not 'bought off' on this issue.

The 'corrupted' model would suggest that the white working class is paid out of super-profits extorted from black labour to play the role of overseers and police for the capitalist class. They would thus be wedded to capital in an unholy alliance to suppress the Africans. But this is not the reality, according to split labour market theory. Rather than willingly accepting a labour aristocracy role, white labour in South Africa has fought against it (much as did Australian labour in closing the ports to cheap Asian labour). They want an economy not based on cheap labour, not having to rely on African labour at all. Apartheid speaks to this ideal, and, naturally, is opposed by capital which wants to make full use of African labour. There is an anti-capitalist idealism in Nationalist policy (even though its immediate consequences are devastating to the African people). Herein may lie a germ of hope.

The basic position of the South African white working class is not one of luxurious corruption, but one of fear for their lives. They are surrounded by enemies, fighting for survival. Their *'laager* mentality' is not just backwoods paranoia. It reflects the fact that there is a potential coalition between capital and African labour which would drive them out. International capital would (I believe) happily dispense with the expensive and troublesome white working class, and directly exploit South Africa's resources and native population.

The key political problem is how to persuade white labour that their ultimate interest lies in a united front with Africans, Indians, and Coloureds against the capitalist class, even if their short-term interest points in the opposite direction. I find myself up against a stone wall on this, believing in my heart that it cannot be done. But here I see an important (if probably ineffectual) role for the intellectual in such a society, namely, the laying bare of the dynamics of the system for all to see. If, for instance, white labour's problem is fully and sympathetically understood (instead of their being treated as either duped or bribed, an unflattering portrait either way), they may be able to achieve a broader perspective on long-term versus short-term interests. By and large white labour in South Africa (and in other racially divided societies) has received a 'bad press' from the intellectual community and this certainly has not helped to broaden their political consciousness.

While split labour market theory can help to expose the dynamics of capitalism which create and perpetuate racial division, it has not yet proven that things would be better under socialism. This is obviously a point of weakness. If white labour cannot be shown that they would be any better off under a different mode of production, it is hard to see why they should be persuaded to join with Africans in the overthrow of capitalism. Further work clearly needs to be done on the effects of socialism on split labour markets. Cursory observation does not provide much basis for optimism.

Any hope for working-class unity in South Africa ultimately depends upon the improvement of the condition of African workers. This may sound circular, but I believe it could be the only possibility. As long as black labour is under the domination of capital, it will continue to be capital's tool, which in turn engenders white labour reaction. Only when the African work force achieves a degree of political strength to free itself from the shackles of capital, will the two segments of the work force be able fully to collaborate with each other and the division between them be healed. This is a formidable problem for African labour, since the natural temptation (as it is for white workers) is to see, not capital, but the other segment of the working class, as the chief enemy; and not without reason. Still there appear to be many African intellectuals and political leaders ready to lead the way toward a socialist ideal, and the recent (1976) uprisings are cause for hope. The general point is: the stronger African labour is, the less threat they pose to white labour, and the greater the possibility of an alliance between them. The gaining of such strength is something only Africans can do for themselves. But the rising surge of the women's movement is evidence that a cheap labour group can develop such strength from within.

In conclusion, I see the political purpose of split labour market theory as follows: first, to help to reveal the true dynamics of the racial order so that people can make realistic choices, and second, to try to show the white working class that its long-term interests lie, not in weakening the African position still further, but in helping to build a strong African labour movement which can withstand capital's predatoriness. The only solution lies in the solidarity of all workers, regardless of race. Needless to say, I am not optimistic that it will come about in the near future.

Notes

I wish to thank Leo Kuper, Barbara Laslett, and Pierre van den Berghe for their helpful comments.

1. For a complete version of this argument, and its supporting documentation, see Bonacich, 1977.

References

Bonacich, Edna 'A theory of ethnic antagonism: The split labor market', *American Sociological Review* (1972) 37 (October), pp. 547-59
——, 'Advanced capitalism and black/white race relations in the United States: A split labor market interpretation', *American Sociological Review* (1976) 41 (February), pp. 34-51
——, 'Capitalism and race relations in South Africa: A split labor market analysis' (unpublished manuscript, 1977)
Kuper, Leo *Passive Resistance in South Africa* (Yale University Press, New Haven, 1957)
——, *Race, Class and Power: Ideology and Revolutionary Change in Plural Societies* (Duckworth, London, 1974)
Kuper, Leo and Smith, M.G. (eds.) *Pluralism in Africa* (University of California Press, Berkeley, 1969)

10 THE POLITICISATION OF ETHNIC UNIVERSITIES: EXPERIENCES WITH SOUTH AFRICA'S 'COLLEGE BREWS'

Kogila A. Moodley

When the Nationalist government of South Africa announced its intention to apply the principle of racial separation to university education in 1957, strong opposition was raised by both politicised blacks and liberal whites. Tribal universities were considered a real defeat for committed white liberal academics such as Leo Kuper, who insisted that all his sociology classes at the University of Natal be racially integrated.[1] These multiracial lecture halls were a political microcosm of South African society where the whole spectrum of positions on South African realities was represented and debated. The subsequent legislation for compartmentalisation of higher education, therefore, spelt the intellectual impoverishment of all groups. It became increasingly evident that the purpose of this legislated segregation was to prevent the exposure of black elites to the liberal ideas of the Kupers and their like, through stricter controls on higher education. The political motivations were clearly articulated by Prime Minister Verwoerd at the time, who pointed to the impact of higher education in heightening the frustrations of the subordinate groups through increasing expectations. It was therefore essential, he maintained, to devise an educational program which would focus on adjusting the gap between black expectations and reality.[2] This was the theme of Leo Kuper's highly perceptive satire, *The College Brew* (1960).

Widespread opposition to separate university education was experienced by the newly established institutions, which were initially only able to recruit a handful of ethnic faculty members. This situation however gradually changed through lack of viable alternatives and separate universities gained greater acceptance. In the case of Indians, perhaps more than other blacks, the more conservative elements saw the ethnic universities as the best of a bad bargain, and harboured the hope that greater opportunities would arise out of them. At the very least, it was hoped, this would mean the provision of new facilities for a few career-oriented academics with no other opportunities for employment inside South Africa.

The impact of segregated higher education is explored here, mainly through the example of the Indian university, after the institution has been in operation for sixteen years. The analysis is based on two years' participant observation as a lecturer at the University College for Indians, now University of Durban-Westville (UDW), from 1965 to 1967 and subsequent extensive interviews with students and faculty between 1972 and 1975 as part of the fieldwork for my PhD dissertation (Adam, 1976). The extent to which the original reservations have been justified, as well as whether the goals of the rulers have been met, is examined.

From the inception, black opinion leaders expressed a number of fears: (1) The isolation of various ethnic groups from one another would lead to ignorance of other groups. Despite its segregated facilities, they argued, the University of Natal and other open universities had provided a milieu for black alliances, where the future African, Indian and Coloured leaders, together with a minority of sympathetic whites could nurture greater understanding of one another. (2) Educational standards would deteriorate. Even the promise of fine buildings, gleaming laboratory equipment and well stocked libraries were considered inadequate, if the principle of 'racial membership' and government control was to be entrenched. (3) Objections were raised to 'Indianisation', with emphasis on Indian languages, Eastern religions and Oriental studies, and 'Africanisation' stressing selected aspects of the cultures as chosen by white administrators. These emphases, they felt, would not only exclude blacks from the mainstream of South African and Western competition, but would heighten intra-communal differences along religious and linguistic lines.

When probed deeper, part of the rejection of separate universities lay in the lack of confidence which blacks had in members of their own group as 'university lecturers', as well as the internalised English prejudices towards 'Afrikaners' as ill-educated and rural folk not used to 'university culture' as colonised blacks had come to know of it.[3] (4) The new universities, it was argued, would not enjoy the autonomy that the open universities did. In the case of Indian education, the Minister of Indian Affairs retained extensive powers, and appointed both the Rector and the Vice Chancellor. All appointments, promotions, salary scales and conditions of service would be subject to the Minister's approval. In addition, where the all-white Council (together with its purely advisory Indian counterpart) had failed to take appropriate actions against a staff member, the Minister was empowered to do so. The Council was to consist of not less than eight persons appointed by the State President, two members of the Senate elected by the Senate, and an Advisory Council consisting of not less than eight Indians, appointed by the State President (Academic Freedom Committees, 1974, pp. 20-1). Such administrative segregation and control, many Indians felt, was a serious danger to critical thought and in general to academic freedom.

Widespread opposition to the University College for Indians was reflected in the terms used at that time to refer to it: 'tribal college', 'bush college', 'concentration camp', 'no-choice university'. In 1961, the student enrolment was only 114, and of the forty faculty members only six were Indians (Horrell, 1962) who were ostracised by sections of the community. Many Indians who could afford it sent their children abroad or influenced their choice of courses to be among those not yet offered by the University, thereby making their children still eligible for enrolment at the open universities. During 1960-1973, 4,618 Indians were admitted to the open universities, as were 81 Africans and 1,077 Coloureds (Academic Freedom Committees, 1974, p. 44). In addition, various attempts to establish alternative private university facilities through the University of London and World University Service were made. Liberal white faculty members of the open universities who were opposed to separate education gave their services in supervising correspondence students. However, the isolation of such students from each other and the lack of viability of such qualifications for obtaining future employment in South Africa led to the reluctant and gradual acceptance of the segregated facilities that were offered.

In 1971, the University College which had up to then been affiliated to the University of South Africa was granted full university status. The University of Durban-Westville (UDW) came into being, again not without fear from some Indian educators who saw the break with the reputable University of South Africa as the final death knell for standards of the community's university education. UDW, by 1974, had five faculties,[4] over fifty departments, and a student enrolment of 2,342 (Horrell, 1976, p. 369). Its new campus and higher *per capita* expenditure on Indian students[5] than on white counterparts makes for incongruity in the South African context, but is a noteworthy stopping point for the official foreign guest to note the efforts of the government in educating its subordinate people 'along their own lines'.

Indeed, much of the earlier opposition to the institution by the community would seem to have disappeared. The scene has changed from non-participation and withdrawal to one of a high degree of involvement on the part of the older generation but not the students. Most Indian educators and community leaders see the University of Durban-

Westville not only as an educational centre, but as a cultural centre for the community, and the paternalistic Rector ensures that 'unique opportunities will be provided for Oriental Studies and research as well as original Indian contributions to Culture, Art and Philosophy' (Ireland, 1975, p. 15).

From the empty halls and boycotted graduation ceremonies of the early sixties, UDW is now, for the most part, well patronised. Indeed, it affords one of the closest contact points between the white ruling group and Indians. The central importance of this institution for present-day Indian aspirations justifies close scrutiny of the earlier apprehensions in the light of the experience of the last decade.

Contrary to the initial assurance that this institution would eventually be staffed by Indians themselves, the evidence was that it became an expedient channel for launching not Indians but Afrikaner graduates into the academic realm. A sizeable number of these appointments constitute promotions for former civil servants. Only 30 per cent of the faculty positions, mostly at the junior level, are presently held by Indians, although there are more than enough qualified Indians who can fill most of these positions.

The idea of 'Indianisation', once reputable in ruling eyes, for distinguishing those in favour of separate education from those who insisted on racially integrated education, has been redefined. Indianisation is now virtually synonymous with 'agitation', since it threatens the positions presently held by whites, and is symptomatic of the anti-white antipathies of the more politicised. An indication of the 'correct line' was articulated by a well entrenched Indian professor and Head of the Department of Psychology at UDW, Professor Ramfol, who called for Indianisation to take its normal course on merit (Graduation Ceremony, May 1974). It was obviously in accordance with official policy since Professor Ramfol was appointed Acting Deputy Rector shortly afterwards. On the other hand, the Council of UDW is now an integrated body, with four Indians and eleven whites; and the Senate, a previously all-white body, in 1974 had 44 whites and four Indians serving on it (Mbanjwa, 1975, p. 168).

The question of whether standards of education have dropped is more difficult to ascertain. In terms of actual content of course material, standards of examinations written, and actual expertise gained, it is widely felt by Indian faculty members in all disciplines in which they are represented that the standards compare very favourably with the so-called 'open' universities. Yet, it is difficult to draw the boundary between course content and the broader aspects of university education.

The segregated university, the lack of choice contrasted with white students', the internalised subordinate-superordinate nature of student-faculty contact, the fear of thinking critically and of articulating non-acceptable thoughts, all strongly influence the attitudes students develop in such situations. The fear of security police 'informants' is inhibiting to students as well as to faculty. Indeed, the passivity of students in lecture halls is poorly explained away by several white members of the faculty as being based on 'the Indian nature' or 'the passive temperament of Indians'. Nor is such 'passivity' alleviated by the humiliation which students feel when the type of dress[6] they should wear is dictated to them, especially when rumour has it that some white administrative staff are supposed to have said 'Indians smell, and *must* therefore keep jackets on at all times!' On an informal level, restrictions were also imposed on white faculty members. One such instance in 1967 was that white women lecturers were asked not to lecture to classes in sandals without stockings. To this, a white faculty member remarked, 'they think we have our sex appeal in our toes!'

On the whole, teaching is very formal. Students complain about un-inspiring lecturers who have little knowledge of the problems blacks face daily and, probably because of difficulties with English as a second language, several lecturers are known to dictate lecture notes from the prepared University of South Africa correspondence lectures. Indeed, formal structures are the only protection in an otherwise uncertain situation. Even Indian lecturers seldom transcend the well-trodden traditional explanations, for fear of being labelled disruptive or revolutionary. Theoretical exploration and social criticism are generally frowned upon in favour of 'doing something for the community'. Though these are by no means mutually exclusive, the focus on micro-level projects, important and immediate though they may be, diverts attention from pertinent questions relating to fundamental conditions of existence in that society and hampers a perspective which can see alternatives to the one-dimensionality of community concerns. Furthermore, it is very different from ideas of local control and community involvement advocated in other societies where there is the possibility for the group to realise its goals. In the South African case, the goals are dictated by government and community involvement essentially means helping to fulfil these official aims. Paternalism is another effective means of maintaining control in such situations, and has the effect of splitting alliances in the subordinate group, since there are always subordinates who are convinced of the 'good intentions' of the white paternal figures. Exploiting traditional parent-child relationships in the Indian community is one way this is done. Selected parents from the traditional elite are frequently called upon to serve in a consultative capacity and, for the most part, never having had the opportunity for higher education themselves, they consider the present generation fortunate for the facilities they have. Hence, they tend to be less critical of the establishment. The following statement by the Rector of UDW is illustrative of this point: 'Many parents have expressed their pleasure that we look after the academic interests of students and do not allow them to get involved in politics' (*The Leader*, 13 June 1969).

The official perspective on student participation was articulated by Professor van der Walt, who was appointed by the State President as the first Chairman of the University College Council in 1961:

> I am convinced that to transfer a political concept of 'democracy' to a university is nonsensical and a 'contradictio in terminis' apart from when it might be applied to students electing fellow students for student affairs only:— and even then not where a spirit of antagonism might prevail by sheer intimidation, and where the desire is not to participate in erecting a humane institution but a revolutionary one. Student Councils are, under such circumstances, completely ineffective, and counter-productive (*Fiat Lux*, May 1972, p. 4).

That students reject this type of control would seem evident in their virtually non-existent organisational life. Even the solitary Debating Society decided to disband 'on principle' in 1969, after it had been denied permission to invite representatives of the Liberal and Progressive Party to address students. The reason given by the Acting Rector in support of the decision was, 'At this stage we don't feel it is appropriate for students to be subjected to these influences ... It is the policy of the College not to allow people who take an active part in politics to address students on the campus' (*The Leader*, 13 June 1969). They were told either to let the university authorities suggest speakers or to select some faculty members to address them instead (ibid.). Similarly, students have constantly resisted the formation of Student Representative Councils, since the University authorities insisted on participation in drafting the constitutions, as well as having faculty representation. Furthermore, like their African fellow students at the African institutions, they felt that they would lay themselves open to police interference. Paternalistic 'supervision' of students has not changed much since

The Politicisation of Ethnic Universities

the establishment of the Indian University. In August 1976, the administration was still reacting to speakers invited by the students. At this time, the Rector warned that only bona fide students, employees of the University and persons who have official business to conduct with the University administration would be allowed on the campus. Students saw this as a direct reaction to speeches made on campus by a former president of the Natal Indian Congress, Dr G.M. Naicker, and a research assistant at the Institute of Race Relations, Mr Gavin Reddy (*Sunday Times*, 15 August 1976).

In 1972, the students at UDW organised a boycott of food and a partial boycott of lectures on 7th and 8th May. Student attempts to draft an SRC constitution were rejected by the University Council, which arbitrarily substituted its own version. The 'revised' document barred affiliation with the South African Students' Organisation (SASO), an all black group espousing black unity and the idea of 'black consciousness', and the National Union of South African Students (NUSAS), the anti-apartheid official student organisation at the English language universities. Student publications and press statements were also prohibited. This was followed by a two day boycott of lectures which the Rector, in his address at the graduation ceremony, attributed to 'the Marxist and Maoist forces of negative and disruptive ideology' which were at work in influencing Indian students (Interview with Secretary of Ad Hoć Committee, also *Leader*, 12 May 1972). In a subsequent student charter, the grievances listed were that there was a vast discrepancy in standards between ethnic universities and the 'open' universities, due to security police activity, informers, the powers of white staff, 'dehumanizing' regulations, the terms of bursary contracts and restrictions on student publications and organisation (*Natal Mercury*, 31 May 1972).

These compaints were reiterated in March 1974 when resident students at UDW under assurance of anonymity publicised charges that their hostel was 'more like a concentration camp than a university residence' (*Sunday Times*, 31 March 1974). They said there were unnecessarily stringent rules governing their lives in the hostel. Several students said that they were personally interrogated by the academic registrar about protest meetings in the residence. They were required to sign a document confirming that they recognised the authority of the house committee and would not engage in contentious matters. Of the 150 students eligible to vote for the house committee, 109 placed blank sheets in the ballot box, but nevertheless the house committee was elected (ibid.). In 1975, students renewed their stance to press for an acceptable SRC constitution. They threatened a boycott of all facilities unless these demands were met (*Sunday Tribune*, 2 February 1975). As in the past, the Rector renewed his offer to meet with students to form an SRC. In response to this a white law professor, subsequently dismissed, is reported to have said, 'Self-respecting students at Durban-Westville University would regard a Student's Representative Council whose constitution was drawn up by the university authorities as puppet representation' (Mbanjwa, 1975, p. 181).

In such situations, unlike the African universities where African faculty members ally with their students against white authorities,[7] Indian faculty members have responded by either being non-committal or by privately supporting the authorities through self-policing.[8] At no time has there been outspoken support for the student cause. Indeed, as in the case of the March 1974 hostel incident referred to earlier, a student who criticised the presence at the meeting of the Indian warden, Professor Ranchod, was subsequently expelled from residence (Mbanjwa, 1975, p. 182).

Such a behaviour syndrome is only partially explained by the prevalent white stereotypes of Indians in South Africa, as being 'opportunistic' and 'lacking backbone'. Three factors seem central for such a phenomenon: (1) The structural context makes 'opportunism' and 'non-committal'/behaviour worthwhile. Simply put, passivity and non-interference are positively reinforced by the establishment and well rewarded by the rulers. (2) Failure to achieve and be upwardly mobile are considered to be the shortcoming of the individual, not a consequence of the situation.[9] In such instances, instead of welding together group members in the face of a ruling group, they are atomised through the demand to be 'successful' at all costs. The prestige and recognition awarded for success, especially in the academic sphere, is extremely high in the Indian community. (3) The relatively privileged position of Indian faculty *vis-à-vis* other members of their group separates their interests from that of students. In the case of African lecturers at geographically isolated institutions, both faculty and students together live outside their traditional community, and the status difference between faculty and student is much lower in view of the degree of dehumanisation which all Africans experience through numerous stringent restrictions on their freedom and mobility. All these factors taken together point to a broader deterioration of educational standards, not only because of any conspiracy to under-educate subordinate groups, nor on account of the actual content of what is taught, but because of the wider political issues involved. The essential gap between white faculty

The Politicisation of Ethnic Universities 125

and black students is unbridgeable under these conditions, and affects the intrinsic value of education for the recipients.

A third major concern of those opposed to separate universities was the isolation of the group, especially from other subordinates. In 1971, it was suggested that 'despite the divergent cultural lines on which segregated education is being conducted, a newer convergence will emerge among people who have shared a common exposure to this colonial type educational experience, and more fundamentally, share in its rejection, (Adam, 1971, p. 212). This prediction would certainly seem to have materialised if the impact of crucial events at all the African Universities since the unrest in Soweto is considered.

At the graduation ceremony of the University College of the North in April 1972, Mr O.R. Tiro, an ex-mineworker and past president of the Turfloop Student Representative Council, whom students elected to represent them, strongly criticised the predominantly white control of black universities, discrimination against black people by the authorities, and the system of Bantu Education in general. He was subsequently expelled by the University's disciplinary committee on 2 May 1972, and when a student petition for his reinstatement was refused, a mass sit-in followed. The Student Representative Council was suspended, all meetings banned, and the police occupied the campus (Horrell, 1973, p. 387; Black Community Programmes, 1972, pp. 174-180).

These events were followed by demonstrations of solidarity by students throughout the country. A meeting of forty black student leaders on 13 May led to a call by SASO for a national boycott by black students on 1 June (*World*, 14 May, *Sunday Express*, 14 May, cited Horrell, 1973, p. 388). On 9 May, students at the University of the Western Cape began a boycott of lectures in support of the students at Turfloop (*Cape Times*, 9 May 1972), followed by a two week boycott by Indian students. Feelings of solidarity were expressed by Indian student leaders who had only shortly prior to this been in confrontation with their own authorities over similar issues. A speaker proposed the boycott motion to a meeting of 1,000 students: 'We are not voting as Indians but as Blacks. We need solidarity to eradicate this repugnant system' (*Daily Dispatch*, 29 May, cited Horrell, 1973, p. 390). Similar boycotts of lectures by Indian students took place at the Springfield Teachers' Training College[10] and the M.L. Sultan Technical College[11] and on other African campuses in support of the Turfloop students.

Whereas some 2,000 residents of Soweto appointed a delegation to negotiate on behalf of the expelled African students, the approach of the Indian parents at UDW was seen quite differently by the students.

Student leaders complained that the parent body 'sold them out' by making counter-deals with the Rector. 'Some members of the parent body who have been politically active in the past, tried to infantilize us by flaunting their "experience" at us'; 'While they told some of us to go on with the strike, they encouraged their own children to return to lectures'. Finally, the Rector promised the parents' body that no disciplinary action would be taken if the strike ended, but a month later four students were suspended for the rest of the year, among them the President of the newly formed council of Presidents of Black SRCs (Horrell, 1973, p. 390).

In general, ethnic universities have politicised and unified black students beyond the expectations of both apartheid ideologues and their critics. A typical example suffices to illustrate this. When students at the University of the North held a pro-Frelimo gathering to celebrate Mozambique's independence in September 1974, and armed police with dogs dispersed them under the Riotous Assemblies Act, accounts of happenings there served as a warning to all black students. One such account by students of the occurrence was:'As the men went past the police, the latter baton-charged them and the students retaliated by throwing small available stones at the police. The women then came back and angrily shouted at the police to stop molesting the men. The police then turned on the women and one was knocked down with a baton blow. The men came to the women's rescue and the police set the dogs on the men, some of whom were now in physical scuffles with the police' (Mbanjwa, 1975, pp. 78-9). What followed was an open declaration of sides between some white faculty members and black students.

In reaction to this deteriorating atmosphere, the Jackson Commission on Africanisation at Turfloop, eight months prior to the pro-Frelimo rallies, recommended that legislation be introduced to give black universities the same degree of autonomy as white universities. The university council, it suggested, should have a black majority and, furthermore, relationships should be established with other South African universities to encourage advanced study and research. As long as complete separation of black and white communities at the universities existed, it was pointed out, the university as an institution could not function satisfactorily. Regarding Africanisation of posts, it was recommended that this should take place at a pace which would not require lowering of standards of teaching and management (Horrell, 1977, p. 371). Subsequent to the pro-Frelimo rallies and unrest in September 1974 at the University of the North, the Snyman Commission was appointed to investigate the causes underlying these developments. Its findings were that the immediate cause of the unrest was extreme hostility to whites, which had been fostered by SASO. This antagonism, Snyman concluded, was further rooted in a deep resentment of the status of whites, exacerbated by the statutory and traditional discrimination against blacks and the humiliation which blacks suffered at the hands of whites (Horrell, 1977, p. 371). The real grievance of blacks was reported to be the manner in which the policy of separate development was executed. Despite these findings, the establishment of separate universities for blacks was seen as a constructive step. Among the recommendations made by the Snyman Commission were (1) as long as the university was not accepted by its people it could not play a fruitful role in the community. Therefore, it was suggested that control of the university be transferred to blacks as soon as possible without waiting for Africanisation of the staff. (2) If the white population, in general, would adopt a more conciliatory attitude toward the blacks, especially the sophisticated blacks, a much better spirit and a greater cooperation would result (*The Star*, WE, 14 February 1976).

It was evident after the rapid spread of support in solidarity with the Turfloop students from all the black universities that separate university education had not succeeded in isolating the concerns and struggles of each campus. Shortly after the publication of the Snyman Report, the Rector of UDW acknowledged that the observations of the Commission applied with equal force to UDW (*Graphic*, 20 February 1976). Unlike the impact of nationalistic views among African students, however, equivalent attitudes among Indian students have much more limited political consequences.

The large-scale and unprecedented 1976 high school disturbances in Soweto heightened dissatisfaction at every black university in the country, revealing even further the failure of ethnically exclusive education to remain uninvolved with wider concerns. In June 1976, the administration buildings and the library at the University of Zululand were burnt down and the university closed for the rest of that year. In Durban, the 'non-white' section of the University of Natal's Medical School held a sympathy march which led to the arrest of 87 black students, a third of whom were Indians. Students at Fort Hare, as on many similar occasions in previous years, held a mass meeting on 17 July to discuss a day of prayer for Soweto (Horrell, 1977, p. 63). This meeting developed into a disturbance and several arson attempts ensued, leading to the university's closure two days later. At the beginning of August, students at the University of the Western Cape decided to boycott lectures for a week. However, when the Rector suspended lectures, students saw this as a betrayal of their cause. This, together with a statement by the all-white staff association dissociating itself from their protest, led to 800 students gathering to block the access road to the campus. Confrontation with the police followed and the administration building was burnt down (Horrell, 1977, pp. 71-2). In a subsequent memorandum to the Rector at the University of the Western Cape, students demanded, among other things, the resignation of the all-white staff association, the opening of the university to other race groups and a fair trial for a student who had been detained under the Terrorism Act. From August to September, unrest in the Western Cape was widespread, throughout high schools and teacher training colleges.

At about the same time, Indian students at UDW held a week long strike in solidarity with students of Soweto. In an open display of their protest, a column of students marched around the university campus urging students in lectures to join a boycott of classes. Their placards read 'Blood Soweto and Tears', 'The Black Man's Blood Flows', 'Stop this Massacre' and 'Our students are being killed'. Several students were arrested, leading to further displays of support.

These examples make it apparent that the ethnic universities are not isolated from each other, contrary to the initial fear of growing ethnocentrism. All institutions without exception have failed to create an uncritical ethnic inclusiveness, of the type which would be compatible with apartheid goals. Indeed, while the self-confidence of segregated ethnic groups has risen in relation to other groups, their wider political sensitivities have not been dulled. This was evident, for example, at the University of Zululand's graduation ceremony in 1975 when Chief Gatsha Buthelezi was awarded an honorary doctorate and some 200 students demonstrated against the 'Bantustan' system. Buthelezi's car was stoned and scuffles ensued between his outside supporters and students. Similar expressions have occurred at UDW toward members of the Indian Council and unsympathetic faculty.

In conclusion, it is evident that separate university education has in several respects achieved the intentions of its political architects. Unlike the open universities, daily personal contacts between students of different ethnic backgrounds cannot flourish. Students spend some of their most valuable years of learning exclusively within their own groups. Many internalise notions of other groups as fostered by apartheid education, since their own experiences are limited not only by university apartheid, but by residential apartheid. Yet surprisingly, in crucial respects, the isolation of university students has led to neither total isolation nor ignorance of one another. The impact of ethnic university structure has in every instance led to a greater politicisation and polarisation between students on the one hand and white faculty and administration on the other. In the process, black students across ethnic lines have become sensitised to each other's problems in spite of a lack of personal contact. Even the ingenious divisive schemes of Indianisation, Africanisation and the like have had little impact on people who were confident of the value of their cultures anyway. If anything, separate universities seem to have given rise to the consciousness of the irrelevance of 'showing the worthiness of one's culture'. It has in the minds of most politicised students become a non-issue. Paradoxically, white faculty members, too, do not remain unaffected; while some come with rigid notions about their students and have these confirmed, there are few who leave unshaken in their convictions about the need for separate education.

Compared with wider political realities, and the university is one of these, the substance of knowledge assumes secondary importance. Students have little respect for those who teach, when they are engaged in upholding a structure preaching human inequality and enjoying its spoils. Under such circumstances, self-determination as a goal assumes priority and all other learning is esoteric. It is not surprising, therefore, that many black students focus on merely 'getting through' the system.

The most noticeable outcomes of separate universities are undoubtedly a broader nationalism and militancy. Hurried attempts to remedy this situation have been made by the government in increasingly appointing black faculty. At three of these colleges there are now black rectors. Furthermore, provisions have been made to open ethnic universities to white students interested in the study of those particular groups and of making it possible for black students to defile the hitherto sacrosanct portals of the Afrikaans universities. An Afrikaans daily sums up the new vision: 'In future there could be a flow of students between different universities, which would show in practice that they are not exclusive, racially-oriented institutions' (*Die Transvaler*, 6 July 1977).

Tribal higher education has come full circle now that its major failure to depoliticise the subordinates into ethnocentric 'community involveent' has become obvious. Contrary to the rulers' designs, ethnic universities backfired in speeding up an anti-white militancy, which would be hard to imagine in integrated liberal institutions imbued with the spirit and praxis of non-racial universalism. However, by appointing black rectors and faculty and diluting the racial exclusiveness, the system may still prevent, for the time being, the ultimate confrontation envisaged in Kuper's satire:

> Umbumbulu is no longer a University College. It was closed after the students' revolt. The Headquarters of the Friendly Territory Advisory Garrison (FTAG) is now established in the College Buildings. The advisory equipment includes tanks, armoured cars, machine guns, sten guns and a variety of flamethrowing devices. Dr. van Tonder is in charge. He was promoted to the rank of Brigadier General in recognition of active service at the College of Umbumbulu, and took over his command after a short and intensive leadership course in the United States of America, sponsored by democrats in that country. He spends most of his time in the memorandum division of the armed forces at the national capital in Pretoria (Kuper, 1960, p. 148)

Notes

1. The Universities of Natal, Cape Town and Witwatersrand had admitted students of all racial groups, even though the University of Natal had always operated a separate 'Non-European Section'. When the Extension of University Education Act was passed in 1959, the University of Natal had an enrolment of 2,679 white students, 50 Coloureds, 489 Asians and 187 African students. The University of Cape Town had 4,471 white, 461 Coloured, 133 Asian and 39 African students, and the University of Witwatersrand, 4,813 white, 30 Coloured, 193 Asian and 74 African students (Horrell, 1962), p. 252.

2. For more extensive treatment of this subject, see K. Adam (1971).

3. These feelings were exacerbated by numerous articulations of anti-Indianism by Afrikaans-speaking politicians, including the first Minister of Indian Affairs.

4. Arts, Science, Commerce, Administration and Law Faculties. In November 1974, it was announced that the Government had decided in principle to establish a medical faculty as well although nothing concrete has yet emerged from this proposal (Horrell, 1976), p. 262.

5. R644 per Indian student, R577 per white, R976 per Coloured and at one African College, R1,490 per African student (Horrell, 1969, p. 211). The duplication of facilities explains these incongruities. Indeed, the 1971-2 figure for Indians is even higher (R1,064), and was caused mainly by the transfer of the University to its new campus (*South Africa*, Indian Affairs, 1973), p. 107.

6. In 1967 men were required to wear jackets at all times and women were not allowed to wear mini-skirts or fancy stockings. While it is recognised that these standards prevail in some private schools in other countries, the informal rationale for these rules together with the societal context adds to the humiliation.

7. As evidenced in the report of a Senior Lecturer from the University of the North at Turfloop (*Rand Daily Mail*, March 1975) and a statement by the principal of the University of the North, Professor Boshoff, to the press, in which he

said, 'the anti-White sentiments of students were encouraged by some members of the Black academic staff' (Horrell, 1975), p. 373.

8. The writer is personally aware of a situation where two Indian faculty questioned an invitation to a prominent and outspoken Indian doctor to address students, on the grounds that the guest had made derogatory statements about the University. Furthermore, students say that the Rector maintains control over who the 'agitators' are through certain known Indian faculty, who they describe as having a 'direct line to the Rector'. Indeed, in an address to the students at the beginning of the academic year, the Rector is reported in the Indian press to have publicly offered 'protection' to 'any student who furnished information about those students who were opposed to extra-curricular activites at the University (*Leader*, 20 February 1976).

9. This is corroborated by the way 'banned' political leaders claim they are shunned by most Indians, as well as random comments by many about such leaders having underestimated the ruthlessness of the whites, and therefore being responsible for their own bannings.

10. All students on strike were suspended and thirteen of them prevented from writing mid-year examinations (*Leader*, 23 June 1972).

11. Three hundred students were suspended (*Leader*, 9 June 1972). One hundred and twenty of them had their bursaries withdrawn, and written apologies were elicited from all of them (*Natal Mercury*, 22 June 1972).

References

Academic Freedom Committees of the University of Cape Town and the University of Witwatersrand, Johannesburg, *The Open Universities in South Africa and Academic Freedom, 1957-1974* (Juta, Cape Town, 1974)

Adam, K. 'Dialectic of Higher Education for the Colonized: The Case of Non-White Universities in South Africa', in H. Adam (ed.), *South Africa: Sociological Perspectives* (Oxford University Press, London 1971), pp. 197-213

——, 'Resistance and Accommodation in a Racial Polity: Responses of Indian South Africans' (Unpublished Ph.D. dissertation, University of British Columbia, 1976)

Black Community Programmes, *Black Review* (Black Community Programmes, Durban, annually)

Gerhart, G.M. 'South African Students' Association (SASO) 1968-1975' (paper presented at the Annual Conference of the African Studies Association, San Francisco, 29 Oct-1 Nov 1975)

Horrell, M. (ed.) *A Survey of Race Relations in South Africa* (South African Institute of Race Relations, Johannesburg, annually)

Ireland, R.R. 'Apartheid and the Education of the Indian Community in the Republic of South Africa', *Plural Societies* (1975), 6, 2, pp.3-17

Kuper, L. *The College Brew* (Universal Printing, Durban, 1960)

Mbanjwa, T. (ed.) *Black Review 1974-5* (Black Community Programmes, Durban, 1975)

Meer, F. 'Indian People. Current Trends and Policies' in P. Randall (ed.), *South Africa's Minorities* (SPROCAS, Johannesburg, 1971)

Walshe, P. *The Rise of African Nationalism in South Africa, 1912-1952* (University of California Press, Berkeley, 1971)

South African Newspapers

Daily News (Argus Group, Durban)

The Natal Mercury (Independent, Durban)
Rand Daily Mail (South African Associated Newspapers, Johannesburg)
The Cape Times (South African Associated Newspapers, Cape Town)
The Star (Argus Group, Johannesburg)
Daily Dispatch (Independent, East London)
Sunday Tribune (Argus Group, Durban)
Sunday Times (South African Associated Newspapers, Johannesburg)

Weeklies

The Graphic (Durban)
The Leader (Durban)
Post (Johannesburg)
The World (Johannesburg)
To the Point (Johannesburg)

Monthlies

South African Outlook (Cape Town)

Government Publications: Government Printer, Pretoria

Fiat Lux, Department of Indian Affairs, monthly.
South Africa, Department of Indian Affairs. Report of the Director of Indian Education, annually.

11 INTELLECTUALS AND ACADEMIC APARTHEID, 1950-1965

Margo Russell

In a paper demonstrating the marked differences in political outlook between English- and Afrikaans-speaking students in South Africa, Danziger (1963) reached the surprising conclusion that intellectuals were not, as Mannheim had supposed, unattached, but biased, committed. An equally plausible conclusion might have been that white South African students were not intellectuals. Among the many divergent definitions of intellectuals, we are offered few which would automatically include students as students, although universities figure prominently as the institutionalised niche for men of ideas.

The assumption that intellectuals are tied closely to universities by employment, certification or reference group needs to be treated with caution. The intellectual stratum, as the term is currently used, is a phenomenon of a particular division of labour, a particular economic system. It might be simply confusing to extend the term to any other phenomenon, but we should not thereby blind ourselves to active intellects which have escaped the university connection (Nettl, 1969, p. 55). The point is particularly important in South Africa where non-Western traditions are curiously strong, both among non-liberal Afrikaners, whose rapidly expanding universities bear but surface resemblance to the European ones, and among the black Africans, caught between pride in their indigenous institutions, and an accompanying repudiation of the colonial institutions, and the unpredictable and often unwanted patronage of an oppressive Afrikanerdom in protecting and fostering these indigenous institutions.

This paper is about students and teachers in South African universities between 1950 and 1965. It attempts to recapture some of the perspectives of the period and to make intelligible some of the responses of those in the universities to the situation in which they found themselves.

Academic fascination with intellectuals is egocentric and introspective. Definitions, usually phrased to include the writer, vary with viewpoint. Yet two elements persist. One is superior mental capacity. In a society where mental capacity has been elevated to the arch-legitimator of inequality, to be intellectual carries for the most part a great deal of social approval. To claim to be intellectual is to be unduly immodest. To describe one's friends as intellectuals is to honour them. The excepting circumstance is where the powerful position achieved through intellect is seen to have become entrenched through the elaboration of theories of society justifying the status quo. 'Bourgeois intellectuals' are despised by radicals for their inability or unwillingness to conceptualise an alternative social order. Yet even here, there is an unwillingness to dismiss 'intellectual' as a simple term of reactionary abuse. Instead the word is redefined, salvaged, purged, reserved for those whose superior mental capacity leads them into politically effective dissent. Indeed the debate about the appropriate referent for the term takes on something of the quality of arguments amongst believers as to the meaning of 'religious'. The exclusive fanatical few deny the authenticity of all who are not of their persuasion, reserving the term for those who are seen to be passionate and zealous (Nettl, 1969, p. 83). The representatives of the establishment are more liberal in their categorisation, placing a high premium on the faithful if uninspired fulfilment of duties prescribed by a higher institutional wisdom (Parsons 1969; Shils 1964).

Even the establishment figures give place in their conceptualisation to dissent, the second persistent element in definitions, and display a loyalty to the foundation usage. Criticism remains a major intellectual activity; intellectuals have 'an inevitable tendency toward negation' (Shils, 1958), 'inherent tendencies to oppose the status quo' and, more strongly, the 'inalienable right of intellectuals to attack (the status quo)' (Lipset, 1960, p. 343, Znaniecki, 1940, p. 370) contrasts the critical reflection about the nature and foundations of the cultural order' with the 'less intellectual' attitudes of conservatives.

But scholarly opinion itself is the outcome of a multitude of factors, not all scholastic. For scholars, academics and intellectuals are also members of government commissions, trade unionists, landowners, aliens, Black Muslims. Lipset and Ladd (1975) have demonstrated the wide range of political views that American academics display. Something of the same diversity is likely to characterise the South African academy, save for one factor: the oppressive society might be expected to evoke by opposition a united front, consolidated by the intimacy which small numbers promote.

The characterisation of South African society as oppressive is a cliche requiring not so much substantiation (for evidence of tyrannical coercion, injustice and cruelty is abundant[1]) as a careful taking apart to see how the burden of oppression is distributed. There would seem to be two elements, objective and subjective. Objectively, oppression may be measured on any one of a range of preferred indices such as denial of freedom of movement, speech, assembly, contract, access, choice and achievement. Although the term lacks the precision which Marxists are able to place on exploitation, it can nevertheless be lent an arbitrary exactness. The subjective element concerns the extent to which such denial is perceived as unjust by persons so deprived.

Those most oppressed objectively are not necessarily the most conscious of oppression. All behaviour is continuously subject to constraints. The definition of some constraints as legitimate, others as illegitimate, is itself a shifting consequence of socialisation. The constraints of adult authority over children in some European societies has recently come to be seen by some as illegitimate; the traditional rights of parents and teachers to coerce is in the process of being redefined as oppression. The eventual legitimacy of this new definition is uncertain. Meanwhile the 'little Red Schoolbook' has been banned in several schools and some countries, and the counter-ideology, that all children can eventually become coercive adults, is being propagated.

Objectively, oppression is not mitigated by a lack of awareness of injustice, but the converse is true; an awareness of injustice heightens oppression by adding to it an extra subjective dimension.

This objective burden of oppression falls squarely on black shoulders in South Africa, with very little differentiation, save marginally for the well-born descendants of chiefs and the highly educated, who have traditionally been exempted from the more irksome curfew, liquor and pass laws. Both these potentially exempted categories are also candidates for consideration as intellectuals in Nettl's terms (1969), being legitimate and competent spokesmen on matters of cultural concern. They represent the black elite of the two cultural streams, the indigenous and the Western. The former have increasingly been patronised by the South African government, and have to a surprising degree been persuaded to assent to the prevailing and proposed political and economic structures.[2] The latter have been a continuing focus of government suspicion, conspicuous for their achievement, despised for their anglicisation, feared for their influence, silenced for their dissent. Their relatively privileged position among other blacks (better conditions of employment, better incomes) is in part outweighed by their acute insight into their situation, above all their deprivation relative to comparable whites. For blacks, awareness of deprivation rises with education. Heightened black political consciousness increases oppression both subjectively, as awareness grows, and objectively as the threat of heightened consciousness is met with new repression. The history of political confrontations in the fifties and early sixties in South Africa was of this pattern of spiralling politicisation and reprisals (Kuper, 1960; 1965, Part 1).

The articulate, educated whites are in a very different situation. Although the very wide powers sought by and granted to the government inevitably threaten their liberties in principle, in practice the vast majority of whites are unaffected by legislation essentially designed to perpetuate their unduly privileged position. It is true that they have no free access to black areas, to black lovers, or to prohibited literature.[3] The right to criticise the existing order is hampered by the ready possibility of banning or worse, under the Suppression of Communism Act.[4] Yet the system gives whites one of the highest standards of living in the world as citizens, one of the highest returns in the world as investors (Adam, 1971, p. 32). The oppressive society presses very lightly on the backs of even the most enlightened whites: an intimidating name-taking at a public meeting; a flutter of indignation at the statutory limitation on the number of resident domestic servants allowed on one's premises; a brief outcry at the violation of private property rights under the Group Areas Act, or of the right to assemble during an emergency. The pressure is rather on the conscience, and here we must recognise the existence of two very distinct utopias, (1) the individualism of Western liberal democracy closely associated with the English-speaking universities, shaping a conscience sensitive to the denial of individual rights; and (2) the collective anti-liberal Afrikaner ideal of secure ethnic identity as the essential framework for individual self-fulfilment, shaping a very different conscience, affronted by policies which disregard the collective identity.

Afrikaner nationalism, initially appealing in its dissent from imperial British orthodoxy, its anti-elitist emphasis on the wisdom and participation of the common man, its pride in the conservation of a despised rural culture, has become increasingly repellent in its authoritarianism, its racialism, and its transformation of the dissenting creed of a defensive minority to the offensive rule of an arrogant minority. Ye system finds its intellectual defenders, who criticise its abuse, urge its reformation, much as *laissez-faire* capitalism finds its intellectual defenders despite the exploitation and poverty which it engenders. The political dissent in Afrikaans universities is very muted, concerned with the refinements of policy about which there is overwhelming consensus.[5]

We might take the extent of white involvement in political dissent as an index of the effectiveness of the English-speaking universities in communicating and propagating the basic tenets of democratic individualism. The record is by and large a poor one, and proves poorer on close inspection than a superficial reading might suggest.

The period of which I have direct experience as a student and teacher conveniently coincides with the National Party's rise to power and the initiation of systematic apartheid policies as distinct from the *laissez-faire* racial discrimination of the earlier period. It is important to see how far the informal structures of racial segregation had already been incorporated into the English-speaking universities at the beginning of this period, not by oppressive governmental decree, but in voluntary conformity with prevailing South African whim and practice. Although the universities of Witwatersrand and Cape Town admitted non-white students to their academic facilities, residential and social facilities were segregated and unequal. The University of Natal extended its inequal and separate facilities to the academic as well as the social sphere, though it retained a common faculty for its segregated campuses. Rhodes University, like the Afrikaans universities, admitted only whites. The University College of Fort Hare, formerly the South African Native College, established by missionary endeavour in 1916, operated an open door policy, but in practice very few whites ever availed themselves of this opportunity. South African universities in 1950 were essentially white institutions. Of the 19,000 full-time students about 1,000 were not white. Of the 2,000 faculty 47 were not white. The statistical picture sixteen years later looked much the same, save for a general expansion. Full-time student numbers had increased to 47,000 of which non-whites were about 3,300; faculty had increased proportionately to some 5,000, amongst whom the blacks had increased from 2.3 per cent (1951) to 8 per cent (1966).[6]

In political terms, however, this had been a period of immense upheaval in the universities as the government had extended to higher education its determined policy of ethnic separation, raising, of course, basic questions of university autonomy, policy and purpose. The superficial continuity in university statistics masks a basic discontinuity in university structure.

The first intimations of the determination of the government to halt the feeble flow of non-whites to the common universities was its suspension in 1951 of government bursaries to African medical students at the University of Witwatersrand, and its concentration of financial support instead to Africans attending the newly established non-white medical campus at the University of Natal (Horrell, 1952, p. 54). Two years later, in December 1953, a commission was appointed to 'investigate and report on the practicality and financial implications of providing separate training facilities for Non-Europeans at Universities'.

This the Holloway Commission reported a year later in February 1955, rejecting (mainly on financial grounds) the establishment of new institutions for blacks, suggesting instead the concentration of Indians and Africans at the existing black campuses of Fort Hare and Natal, and the integration of Coloureds and all postgraduates into the existing 'white' universities. Within two months of receiving the Commission's Report, the Minister of Education, Arts and Science announced the Government's intention, nevertheless, to segregate the universities, and an interdepartmental committee was appointed to advise the government thereon. By the time its findings and recommendations were published as the 'Interdepartmental fact-finding committee on the financial implications in connection with the establishment of separate University Colleges for Non-Europeans' (*White Paper* C 1957), the Separate University Education Bill, March 1957, for the establishment of the 'tribal colleges' was already before parliament and opposition to the legislation was in full cry.

Yet early white reaction to the government's consistent declaration of its intentions was slow and muted. The Nationalist Party's juggernaut determination and strength had not yet been fully demonstrated. The complacency of English-speaking South Africans that good sense in the long run must prevail had not yet been shaken. Africa was still a colonial territory; Ghana was still the Gold Coast; the Mau-Mau were stirring up trouble in Kenya; and Seretse Khama had been banished from Bechuanaland for marrying a white woman. The sharp choices which were later to be seen to be confronting whites in Africa were still vague. The new Liberal Party formed in South Africa in 1952 with its mild advocacy of a qualified non-racialist franchise was perceived as so eccentrically interracial that its three candidates in the Natal Provincial elections in 1953 had between them secured only 385 votes (Horrell, 1954, p. 6). In the long term, good sense must prevail.

The South African Institute of Race Relations reacted early by sponsoring a conference in May 1954 on the 'concept of a University and its function in a multiracial society' attended by representatives of university convocations, staff, student representative councils, churches, the National Union of South African Students and others, including the Afrikaans Bureau of Racial Affairs, who, along with the Afrikaans University of Potchefstroom, dissented from the conference conclusion that 'a university is the centre for the preservation and advancement of learning for its own sake and its dissemination to all who are academically qualified for admission' on the grounds that it paid insufficient attention to the attitudes and traditions of the country in which the university functioned (Horrell, 1954, p. 109).

The Institute of Race Relations in its annual survey doubted whether segregated black universities, denied 'opportunity for normal contacts with Europeans', would be able to give 'a sound humanistic education', particularly to Africans who 'had no equivalent in their traditions to Western forms of scholarship' (Horrell, 1954, p. 108). No anxieties were expressed about the quality of humanistic education in the traditionally segregated white universities. The white students at the University of Natal reaffirmed their opposition to participating in a multiracial graduation ceremony with black graduands (Kuper, 1965, pp. 143-66).

Beyond the universities the African, Coloured and Indian Congresses, recovering from the disintegration of the Campaign against Unjust Laws (Kuper, 1956), were planning a Congress of the People for 1955 to determine the future of South Africa; the police had started taking the names, addresses and photographs of participants at political rallies, a practice which was criticised for creating 'a psychological effect of wrongdoing' among 'the more moderate and responsible European sympathizers, who might otherwise have given the Congress of the People Movement a more constructive direction' (Horrell, 1954, p.15). A similar criticism was raised against the new practice of 'banning' under the Suppression of Communism Act, in terms of which the 'more moderate leadership' had been rendered politically impotent. The Reservation of Separate Amenities Act of 1953 had established the legality of unequal separate facilities for different races, and the Bantu Education Act had established the principle of education as an allocative tool of manpower resources and not a universal human right to self-fulfilment.

It was not until mid-1956 that the universities began to react to the possible implications of the government's plans for them. Two issues were closely intertwined; the first was racial segregation upon which faculty and student opinion was very lukewarm. The second was university autonomy upon which there was a much readier consensus. Not only was the principle understood and enshrined in the Western academic tradition, but the issue readily evoked all the dormant anti-Afrikaner feeling which is very much part of the South African English academic tradition. 'They' were trying to push 'us' around.

The terms of opposition were carefully phrased, from the more radical National Union of South African Students, who at their July 1956 congress launched a campaign to 'oppose interference with the principle of *academic* non-segregation', and the University of Witwatersrand where in September 1956 at a student meeting only 51 people opposed the 1,300 who voted against 'the *compulsory* introduction of apartheid' (my emphasis), to the more cautious University of Cape Town, who merely affirmed support for full university autonomy by 1,144 votes to 15. A resolution of support for the 'Open Universities' was passed by a general meeting of white students of the University of Natal in 1956 only after protracted debate and assurance that it was autonomy not racial integration, which was being supported. Rhodes University sent 'a message of encouragement' to the Open Universities Liaison Committee (Horrell, 1956, p. 205). The ethnic loyalties which rallied reluctant support among the English probably inhibited any potential support among Afrikaans academics who might equally have been moved by the issue of autonomy though not of racial segregation.[7]

In December 1956 the Convocations of Witwatersrand and Cape Town met to protest, and in January 1957 the Universities of Cape Town and Witwatersrand held a joint conference in Cape Town on open universities. Students of these two institutions organised placard-carrying demonstrations at their University entrances, 'Keep These Gates Open'. The National Union of South African Students naively appealed to the public to oppose the introduction of politics into learning, a slogan which had already earned it the ostracism of the black campus at Fort Hare, and which it was shortly to jettison in favour of radical student participation (Legassick and Shingler, 1968, pp. 133-4).

The Separate University Education Bill was published in March 1957 proposing the cessation, forthwith, of admission of non-white students to the existing universities without the consent of the Minister, and empowering the assigned Ministers to establish new ethnic university colleges for non-whites, to be governed by councils appointed by the Governor General. The assigned Ministers were to have power to appoint staff and senate, to prescribe departments, to establish the powers, privileges and duties of all staff including the principal. In their hands also lay the power to promote, transfer and discharge staff, and to admit students. Lest the Ministers exercise these powers too benignly, the Bill took the precaution of defining 'misconduct', in seventeen sub-clauses, to include 'insubordination', 'adverse public comment on the administration of a government department', and the propagation of 'any idea ... prejudicial to the administration of any university college or government department' (Horrell, 1957, pp. 199-200). Punishment for misconduct ranged from fines through demotion to discharge. The Bill also, fatally, made provision for the transfer of Fort Hare and the Natal medical school to government. It had subsequently to be withdrawn on the technicality of being hybrid, but not before both government and opposition had shown their hands and their relative strength.

The Councils and Principals of the open universities petitioned that they be heard at the Bar of the House in opposition to the Bill, but the motion that they be heard was not even debated (Horrell, 1957, p. 201). Spokesmen within the House couched their opposition in conservative rather than radical terms, 'violations of the traditional and accepted practices of civilized society'. There was a quaint echo of the genteel nineteenth century in the outrage of another speaker at 'this curious plan of balancing university courses with available jobs' which was 'the most extraordinary interpretation of a university' (Horrell, 1957, p. 206). Outside parliament similar views dominated the white opposition who argued how important it was that 'non-white students should have campus and lecture room contact with European students whose cultural background has trained them in the Western tradition of learning which was lacking in indigenous African society'. All-black universities, it was gloomily predicted, would foster 'an exclusive nationalism' (Horrell, 1957, p. 198).

Exclusive nationalism was, however, the avowed government intention. The ethnically exclusive universities were envisaged as exercising an 'important formative influence' on 'underdeveloped national groups' (Horrell, 1959, pp. 271-272). In submitting the revised, legally viable Extension of University Education Bill a year later in August 1958, and the University College of Fort Hare Transfer Act in 1959, government spokesmen argued that 'open or mixed universities will never be able to meet the real requirements of the Non Europeans . . . (they) will give them an alien and contemptuous attitude towards their own culture . . . If we are in earnest about creating a future for the Bantu, the establishment of their own university colleges is imperative'. The black graduate 'should seek and find his highest fulfilment in the environment of his own social group' (Horrell, 1958, p. 200). Emphasis on the individual, so central an aspect of English university education, was to be replaced by an emphasis on the group. Thus Fort Hare had become 'nothing but an English university for non-Whites . . . The needs of the Xhosa community as a whole had not been taken into account' (Horrell, 1959, p. 272).

While the English academics were urging that blacks should not be denied opportunities to acquire, through contact, the culture of whites which would give them the 'fructifying contacts with a wider universal culture' (Horrell, 1959, p. 274), the Afrikaner academics were urging a speedier implementation of separate development, the national independence of black states, and a closer consultation with black opinion, including 'rebels and agitators, not chiefs who are the hirelings of the government' (Horrell, 1958, pp. 16-18). The government quickly disociated itself from the views of these 'parlour intellectuals', and in April 1958 Verwoerd resigned from the academic Bureau of Racial Affairs.

Yet Afrikaners, academics and legislators, remain highly cohesive in their conviction of the moral rectitude of racial separation and in their opposition to liberalism. In its enlightened form, Afrikanerdom urges instant full realisation of the promise of independence for each ethnic group. In its more sinister and reactionary form it expounds a rigid cultural imperialism, rather than independent development for blacks.

> We believe that God ... has willed separate nations and peoples and has given each separate nation and people its particular vocation ... We accept the principle of the trusteeship of the White man, namely the Afrikaner over the non-White ... We believe that only when the Coloured man has been christianized can and will he be truly happy ... and secure against his own heathen and all kinds of foreign ideologies ... We believe that the teaching and education of the native must be grounded in the life and world view of the Whites more especially of the Boer nation.

This doctrine is the explicit basis of one of the Afrikaans universities. The University of Potchefstroom for Christian Higher Education expressly omits in its constitution the 'freedom of conscience' clause, and follows instead the doctrinaire principle that

> instruction and practice in the secular sciences must proceed from the Christian life and world view ...
> We believe that our university education can only be complete if the right men and women stand at the wheel ... University councils have no more serious vocation than to appoint the right men and women ... the professors and lecturers must be convinced Christian and National scientists.[8]

A similar foundation was urged for the black ethnic universities. A 'religious foundation' was explicitly recommended (Horrell, 1958, p. 198). Far from guaranteeing the traditional freedom of conscience, their constitutions incorporated a demand for obedient consensus by staff and students which is the antithesis of the Western tradition; many faculty posts have been designated 'State posts' and are an integral part of the civil service.

Intellectuals and Academic Apartheid

The Bill made its stormy way through parliament. The opposition, momentarily finding direction in its heroic role defending the prestigeful Western institution of university autonomy, responded to the governmental guillotine on the debate by forcing divisions on every clause and amendment. Yet the outcome was so much a foregone conclusion that even while the debate raged, building work had already begun on the new campuses for Venda, Shangaan and Tsonga at Turfloop (now the University of the North, Sovenga), for the Zulus at Ngoya (now the University of Zululand, Empangeni), and for Coloureds outside Cape Town (now the University of the Western Cape, Kasselsvlei). Fort Hare, *alma mater* of several generations of Southern Africa's black elite, was scheduled to pass into government control and into Xhosa student monopoly on 1st January 1960. Indignation at the proposed metamorphosis led several Fort Hare faculty members to resign, and precipitated the dismissal of several others, including seven white heads of department. 'I will not allow a penny of any funds of which I have control to be paid to any persons who are known to be destroying the Government's policy of apartheid.' Thus the Minister (Horrell, 1959, p. 277).

The faculty at the new black institutions are predictably Afrikaaners, and though black graduates are being assimilated as staff, there was in 1973 marked impatience from the black community that this was not happening fast enough (Horrell, Horner and Hudson, 1974, pp. 370-4). The facilities, purpose built, and mocked for their incorporation of what the architects fancied were traditional ethnic features – such as an open air common 'room' with central open fireplaces – are nevertheless vastly superior to the segregated facilities which had been offered, for example, by the University of Natal to its black non-medical campus, which for several years was a rented warehouse.

The student/teacher ratio in the new institutions after five years was a favourable 5:1, reflecting the shortage of appropriately qualified students.[9] Africans, for example, with the monopoly of three of the new ethnic colleges as well as a substantial share of the medical school at Natal, and comprising fifteen million persons in 1966, had only 2,034 candidates attempting the matriculation examination in that year, of which only 23.9 per cent were successful (Horrell, 1968, p. 222). The state expenditure *per capita* on the new colleges was understandably very high: R1, 221 per annum at the University of the North and R2,145 at Fort Hare in 1964, compared with a mere R483 in the old universities (Horrell, 1968, p. 223), a reflection of their relative age and also of the government's priority for ideological over short-term economic strategies.

Educated black reaction to the new universities shared some of the indignation of English-speaking academics, tempered by practical consideration of various kinds; the repressive elements in the new institutions were to affect them not in principle but in practice. Their protests when they made them were not so much the refined intellectual arguments about principle but bold statements about themselves as the selected, highly achieving few.

> Let it be noted once and for all that our stand as students of Fort Hare and as future leaders of our country, upholding the principles of education as universally accepted, remains unchanged and uncompromising . . . our outright condemnation of University apartheid legislation remains steadfast (Horrell, 1959, p. 277).

For blacks wanting academic qualifications, options were very limited. There was no great enthusiasm for a boycott. The aggressive vigour which black student organisations in the new institutions have since displayed suggests that students have not been recruited from the quiescent few, but are from the representative majority, who had watched the noisy protest at the government seizure of black schools in 1954 fade into resigned acceptance of the things which cannot be changed.[10] The Nationalist Party's single-minded determination and power were better appreciated in 1959 than in 1954, as were the limitations of the power of peaceful protest and persuasive argument to convert Afrikanerdom to liberal multiracialism. Some took advantage of the new opportunities for academic employment. For others there were the millenarian distractions of more popular political involvement, for 1960 was a year of surging black optimism, when for a brief moment far-reaching change seemed imminent through the sheer momentum of awakening black demands. Even *The Times* of London was momentarily misled ('South Africa's Revolution is in its third day') in April 1960. By the time the government had re-established its grasp on the situation there were few who would have ranked university autonomy high on any inventory of assailed rights in South Africa.

There seemed something inherently futile in continuing to plead for the preservation of the familiar contours of this one Western institution in a society in which so many other equally valued Western institutions were being systematically dismembered. The confrontation between the authoritarian Afrikaner government and the *laissez-faire* tradition which had preceded it, and which had shaped the expectations of a generation of black and white non-Afrikaners, was sharpening.

Reactions varied. Many English-speaking whites reoriented themselves to explicit alliance with Afrikaners. Several, perhaps several hundred black intellectuals were arrested.[11] Many of the best academics left the country and many second-best academics gratefully stepped into their places, surprised and pleased at their sudden promotion, not yet cognisant of how the replenishing international flow of visiting academics, so stimulating a feature of the fifties, had already dried up.

Although the Extension of University Education Act had prohibited the attendance of non-whites at the old white universities except with the express permission of the Minister, this permission continued to be fairly widely given; the number of blacks at white universities has remained remarkably constant. There has been if anything a slight increase in interracialism in the old universities. For, having established the legality of the principle of unequal facilities for different race groups, the government, swayed doubtless by economic and manpower considerations, has nevertheless admitted blacks to white universities to study those subjects not available at their own ethnic colleges. Even the Afrikaans University of Potchefstroom in 1974 had six black students. Interracialism was accelerated by the University of Natal desegregating its non-medical campus shortly after the 1959 Act, and by an extension of the rights of black students within the universities of Cape Town and Witwatersrand.

Yet the decade of heroic campaigning by English universities for the lifting of race restrictions on their campuses which followed the 1959 Act has a certain hollow ring about it. Those who bolted the stable door after the horse had fled, although not the horse thieves, look suspiciously like their accomplices. The government's iron intention to limit and control black student numbers in white institutions provided a reassuring context for noisy English declarations about the new-found desirability of university desegregation. The tradition of campaigning for racial integration at Cape Town and Witwatersrand has now become institutionalised, something of an end in itself. Each year a new cohort of campaigners is recruited from the undergraduates, supported by sufficient faculty to lend the issue dignity, opposed from time to time with sufficient rash hostility by the police to give a semblance of real political action (Horrell *et al.*, 1974, p. 375). Much of this popular English student anti-government protest can probably be attributed to anti-Afrikaner, as much as pro-black, sentiment. Several demonstrations have ended up as confrontations between English- and Afrikaans-speaking students. The Cape Town students' sit-in, protesting at their

Council's decision in August 1968 to rescind on racial grounds the new appointment of a black, Dr Mafeje, to a senior lecturership in the Department of Social Anthropology, was brought to an end by the physical intervention of students from the Afrikaans University of Stellenbosch. Picketing students at Witwatersrand in that same year were pelted with eggs, fruit and whitewash by students from the new Rand Afrikaans University, and later a deputation of students from Witwatersrand were 'manhandled' by students from the University of Pretoria, while delivering a petition to the Prime Minister (Horrell, 1968, p. 264).

Yet political participation from whatever motivation may itself be a transforming experience. What begins as a temperate and moderate defence of university autonomy can, in the face of government intransigence, steadily become a more radical demand. By 1974, placard-carrying students were demanding, not the right to determine their own university admissions policy, but the release of political prisoners and those who had been banned and detained for active opposition to apartheid and white domination (Horrell *et al.*, 1974, p. 375). The radicalisation of the National Union of South African Students can be understood in these terms (Legassick and Shingler, 1968). Radical political socialisation is only one among many possibilities and, although not typical, it is common enough among academics to merit analysis.

In the fifties the mood of black students was conciliatory. When, for example, at the segregated University of Natal, a white Christian student society invited cross-campus participation, black student attendance at white campus meetings was embarrassingly high in contrast to white indifference, perhaps a reflection of missionary monopoly of black high schools, perhaps a curiosity about how the other half lived. Whatever their motives, black students were very ready to establish links with white students. Even when their political allegiance dictated non-cooperation with whites, as for example the Non-European Unity Movement, described by Kuper as exercising an influence disproportionate to its numbers on the black non-medical campus at Natal (1946, p. 155), their personal inclinations were to dialogue and debate, even occasionally to dinner parties ('But don't tell the others, they'll *donder* me for socialising with a liberal').

In the fifties, liberalism was radical. Liberal criticism, the hallmark of the moderate fulfilment of expectations in the Western academic tradition, became in South Africa a threat to the *status quo*, and those who exercised it were seen as dangerous and labelled trouble makers. Thus defined, they found themselves, in the thinly peopled intimacy of white South African society, pushed willy-nilly into the embrace of the less moderate Marxists, Trotskyists and others, one of a small cadre of dissenters, expected to proclaim and protest, defend and defy. By infection such people became radical. By situation they remained moderate; wide police powers rendered minor moderate acts of opposition punishable, and although these powers were rarely invoked[12] their existence lent moderate acts an air of daring. The political consequences of this moderate liberalism were different for whites and blacks. White liberals addressing themselves to white audiences were innocuous; their appeal was inherently limited. Black liberals addressing themselves to black audiences were dangerous, since their appeal was wide and its consequences disruptive. The inequalities of black and white against which liberals saw themselves pitched were as marked in the political sphere as in all others.

The hardening of black attitudes in the sixties, heralded by new Africanist dissension in the African National Congress, the rise of the Pan African Congress with its greater racial appeal, and, on the student front, the establishment of exclusively black student organisations, the African Students Association, the African Students Union of South Africa and later the South African Students Organization, posed acute problems for the liberal intellectual whites. Right-wing white rejection of liberalism had been a salve to the liberal conscience, assuaging chronic guilt at being privileged whites. Radical black rejection was more disconcerting. The white position was akin to that of the radical bourgeois intellectual in Europe, but more starkly and uncomfortably compromised by the contradiction between privileged life style and theoretical opposition to the social arrangements which made it possible. The intellectual in Europe may be able to persuade himself that his position is achieved, his status deserved, the reward of talent and effort. The ascribed element in his situation is at least partially obscured by a system which officially denies its existence. The white South African academic cannot escape the knowledge that his position is overwhelmingly ascribed. He is in the first instance a white. Something of his unequal opportunity to achieve his double privileged position is reflected in the fact that his chances of becoming an undergraduate in 1972 were 820 times greater than those of an African.[13]

It was guilt at this situation which in the early sixties drove many young white academics into the extremism of sabotage (Legassick and Shingler, 1968). The pressures on whites rather than blacks to take this dramatic action were very strong. Whereas blacks could self-righteously and self-interestedly assume their allegiance with the underdog, could even be condoned for total political withdrawal, the whites had to prove themselves. Their choice, among alternative analyses of the situation, was for those carrying immediate implications for action rather than for any evolutionary framework, the adoption of which was to risk being dismissed as an opportunist and a hypocrite. The pressure to do and to be seen to be doing probably also accounted for the speed with which the police were able to infiltrate the sabotage movement and eliminate it. The severe sanctions in themselves provided the cathartic opportunity for public affirmation of allegiance. The emotional appeal of sabotage outweighed its strategic irrationality. With the passing of the sixties, government opposition to incipient liberalism in the universities had hardened, provoking a more determined counter-opposition on the part of some, yet in a context of increasingly authoritarian control over universities, which is more and more taken for granted within South Africa, though it may surprise outsiders.[14]

By holding its purse strings tighter, and tying its subsidies to the fulfilment of stipulated conditions[15], the government has succeeded in rendering university councils more biddable to its demands. Although the Western tradition is thereby flouted, the abiding tie between the universities and what Shils memorably calls 'the Mighty' remains intact. The tension between the Afrikaner and English conceptions of the proper role of a university reminds us that universities are not the eternal repositories of truth, essential to every society, transcending social circumstances, which they are often persuasively represented to be by those anxious to legitimate a system which offers them great privilege; they are culturally specific. The institutionalisation of social criticism by the universities in the West is a historically unique by-product of a particular polity and a particular form of educational selection which guaranteed that the criticism would not exceed certain bounds. Western universities have their autonomy because they exercise it predictably. In more centralised political systems the role of the universities is more circumscribed. The social critical function of the university is discouraged, and easily divorced from its technological exploratory function. Ideas of scope are encouraged; ideas of quality require careful control (Lipset and Ladd 1975, pp.72-3). These are the very conditions under which Nettl suggests intellectuals paradoxically flourish; when their 'social role . . . is inhibited . . . strongly and directly.' (1969, p. 120).

Nettl's intellectual is a very pure combination of theoretical insight and political effective commitment. Ideally the commitment is to the ideas, the action flows from the intellect. The South Africa data suggest that the action flows from social location rather than from ideas. The black elite is drawn into the political struggle through ethnic group membership. It is the experience of being black rather than ideas of what ought and could be, which determine black political affiliation. The ground swell of popular black resentment carries the educated with it rather than relying on the educated to mobilise support by articulating dissent. Black university students responded to the political disturbances in Johannesburg in June 1976 by imitation; within two days of the outbreak of arson and violence in Soweto following police shootings of school pupils on June 16th, university buildings, including libraries, at the campuses at Empangeni and Sovenga had been burned. On 17 July a similar attempt failed at Fort Hare and the University was closed indefinitely after police had been called in. On 4 August the Faculty of Commerce and Law Buildings at Kasselsvlei were destroyed by petrol bombs. Superficially at least it seemed the black intellectuals were bent on the destruction of all educational symbols as well as resources. But the new black radicalism of the seventies and the role of intellectuals in it require a more penetrating analysis. The school students who initiated and sustained the 1976 rebellion are in many ways analogous to university students in other countries, in terms of age, selectivity and raised expectations. Like black university students, they are members of the South African Student Organization. The articulate educated dissent; the form it took had all the blind fury of the inarticulate.

The basis for black political involvement is not necessarily the universal; political spoils are surely as compelling as utopian ideals. Opportunism vies with idealism in prompting political participation. A similar pressure of group expectations and material interests makes for the political passivity of most English white academics. They should not be judged too harshly. Western academics in a liberal society exercise their critical capacities in safe conformity to institutionalised demands; indeed their prestige may be seen to be enhanced by this very activity, provided always that they do not exceed the bounds of what is seen to be reasonable criticism. In South Africa the threshold for reasonable criticism is very low. Few academics jeopardise their position by exceeding it.[16] The consequences are very different for people in different institutions. The Afrikaner professors at Potchestroom who in 1959 gave interviews to the press, criticising government apartheid policies as disregarding the feelings of non-whites, were severely sanctioned by a special meeting of their university council for 'careless and undignified exercise of their right to freedom of speech'. The effectiveness of this form of sanction among Afrikaners is evidenced in the professors' apologetic response (Horrell, 1959, p. 25). Similar sentiments from English whites at Fort Hare in the same year led to their dismissal, while at English-speaking universities teachers may be feted for such expressions.

Sociologists have shown a remarkable tenacity in defending the plausibility of the notion of privileged insight which their discipline affords. They will probably cling with equal tenacity to the idea of the intellectual as one whose privileged insight, flowing from scholarship, will, through his integrity, lead him to dissent in accordance with this insight. Meanwhile the world is filled with people whose multiple affiliations will continued to pull and push them, often in contradictory directions at the same time. White academics trained formally in the liberal Western tradition will be peculiarly subject to cross-pressures. The academic's ability to frame consistent policies in terms of an overarching idea is not surprising (Lipset and Ladd, 1975, p.39); his ability to act consistently in line with that idea would be altogether more unusual unusual.[17] Academics in South Africa, black, Afrikaner and English white, play out their respective roles as blacks, Afrikaners and English-speaking whites. In this, they are probably not as different from Americans, Britons and Europeans as we might at first imagine.

Notes

1. The International Commission of Jurists' report, *South Africa and the Rule of Law* (1960). Appendices contain particularly horrifying, legally attested evidence of cruelty.

2. The line between persuasion and coercion is notoriously hard to draw. Many chiefs were deposed for dissent. See Carter, Karis & Stultz (1967).

3. Censorship presumably particularly affects the intellectuals, and is exercised under the Suppression of Communism Act 1950 the Internal Security Act 1976 and by the Publications Control Board. 'Undesirable publications' as defined by the *Report of the Commission of Enquiry in Regard to Undesirable Publications* (U.G. 42/1957) are 'those that would be deemed . . . offensive or harmful by . . . the ordinary decent reasonable and responsible inhabitant of the Union'. Particularly ironic is the banning of publications which 'engender friction or feelings of hostility between various population groups'. No government publications have yet fallen under the heavy hand of the censor, though Jacobsen's *Index of Objectionable Literature* runs to 305 pages of small print on books alone. See *The Times*, London, 7 June 1976.

4. On 10 June 1976 the Internal Security Act extended the provisions of the Suppression of Communism Act of 1950 to include the banning, suppression and detention of organisations, publications and persons 'expressing views or conveying information, the publication of which is calculated to endanger the security of the state or maintenance of public order' without their having been

found to be 'communistic'. Moving the second reading of the Bill, the Minister of Justice singled out 'the student front', along with 'the labour front', as a potential source of trouble requiring preventive detention. The first person to be banned under the enacted legislation was Fatima Meer, a South African Indian sociologist (Keesings Contemporary Archives 27932A).

5. The pressures of conformity were nicely articulated by Dr A. Hugo of the University of Stellenbosch in a letter to *Die Burger*, 2 June 1959, when he complained that to express any divergent opinion was to be 'immediately stamped as a person who had fallen by the way' (Horrell, 1958), p. 25.

6. Figures from *South African Statistics 1974*, Government Printer, Pretoria, pp. 5.2-5.9. Figures on Coloured and Indian faculty not available.

7. The minority report of the *Commission of Inquiry into Separate Education* (U.G. 32/1958) (para. 9, 10) cited the Afrikaner Bureau of Racial Affairs and the Afrikaans University of Potchefstroom as rejecting the principle of State control of universities. See Horrell (1958), p. 194.

8. Christian National Education. A mimeographed translation of an Afrikaans pamphlet circa 1956, Art. 6(6), 14, 15.

9. In fact the Universities accept unmatriculated students for a variety of diploma courses, in administration, social work, theology, nursing, and librarianship *inter alia*. In 1964 more than a third of all students were unmatriculated nondegree students. See *Bantu Education Journal*, October 1966.

10. The events in South Africa since 1976 suggest a determined renewed rebellion against Bantu Education.

11. According to the Minister of Justice (12 July 1960) 1,813 non-whites and 94 whites had been detained between April and June 1960, of which 1,200 had been released without charge by mid-July (Horrell, 1960), p. 79.

12. I have in mind the heavy fines for the possession of banned literature, in principle levied for possession of Marx, in practice, for political pamphlets.

13. White students are 1.64% of their race group. African students are 0.002% of their race group. Figures from *South African Statistics 1974* (5.2, 5.6, 1.5).

14. For example, the Principal of the University of Natal in 1967 suspended the entire Students Representative Council and debarred its members from ever participating in non-academic student affairs, as a reprisal for the publication in a campus newspaper of a derogatory article about himself (Horrell, 1967), p. 285.

15. The University Amendment Act 24 of 1968, and the subsequent Commission of Enquiry, appointed September 1968 to recommend, *inter alia*, the basis for subsidisation in white university education (Horrell, 1968), p. 253.

16. There are some, however. On 13 November 1975 a 30-year-old white law lecturer at the University of Natal was sentenced to 7½ years imprisonment under the Suppression of Communism Act, for recruiting for unlawful activities two persons (who turned state evidence). He said, 'I cannot ever accept that it is wrong to act as I have done, for freedom and equality, for an end to racial discrimination and poverty' (Keesings Contemporary Archives, 27610).

On 29th September 1975 a white lecturer in political science at the University of Cape Town was sentenced to seven years under the Suppression of Communism Act for preparing and distributing subversive pamphlets (Keesing, 28010).

17. Lipset and Ladd found that 'highly productive academics who endorse liberal programmes in the national arena reacted negatively to many campus protests ... which they saw threatening ... their own positions as custodians and beneficiaries of this "idea of a university" '(1975), pp. 216-17.

References

Adam, H. *Modernizing Racial Domination*, (California University Press, Berkeley, 1972)
Carter, G., T. Karis and M. Stultz *South Africa's Transkei: The Politics of Domestic Colonialism* (Heinemann, London, 1967)
Danziger, K. 'Ideology and Utopia in South Africa' *British Journal of Sociology* (1963), 14, pp. 59-76.
Horrell, M. *A Survey of Race Relations 1951-52* (South African Institute of Race Relations, Johannesburg, 1952)
———, *A Survey of Race Relations 1953-54* (South African Institute of Race Relations, Johannesburg, 1954)
———, *A Survey of Race Relations 1955-56* (South African Institute of Race Relations, Johannesburg, 1956)
———, *A Survey of Race Relations 1956-57* (South African Institute of Race Relations, Johannesburg, 1957)
———, A Survey of Race Relations 1957-58 (South African Institute of Race Relations, Johannesburg, 1958)
———, *A Survey of Race Relations 1958-59* (South African Institute of Race Relations, Johannesburg, 1959)
———, *A Survey of Race Relations, 1959-60* (South African Institute of Race Relations, Johannesburg, 1960)
———, *A Survey of Race Relations 1967* (South African Institute of Race Relations, Johannesburg, 1967)
———, *A Survey of Race Relations 1968* (South African Institute of Race Relations, Johannesburg, 1968)
———, D. Horner and J. Hudson *A Survey of Race Relations 1974* (South African Institute of Race Relations, Johannesburg, 1974)
International Commission of Jurists *South Africa and the Rule of Law*, (Geneva, 1960)
Kuper, L. *Passive Resistance in South Africa*, (Cape, London, 1956)
———, 'The heightening of racial tensions', *Race* (1960) 11 l
———, *An African Bourgeoisie* (Yale University Press, New Haven, Connecticut 1965)
Legassick, M. and J. Shingler 'South Africa' in D. Emmerson (ed.), *Students and Politics in Developing Nations* (Pall Mall, London, 1968)
Lipset, S.M. *Political Man* (Heineman, London, 1960)
Lipset, S.M. and E.C. Ladd *The Divided Academy* (McGraw Hill, New York, 1975)
Nettl. J.P. 'Ideas, intellectuals and the structures of dissent' in P. Rieff (ed.), *On Intellectuals* (Doubleday, Garden City, New York, 1969)
Parsons, T. 'The intellectual; a social role category', in P. Rieff (ed.), *On Intellectuals* (Doubleday, Garden City, New York, 1969)
Shils, E. 'The intellectuals and the powers', in *Comparative Studies in Society and History* (1958) 1, p. 8
———, 'Intellectuals' in Shils (ed.), *Encyclopaedia of the Social Sciences*, vol. 7 (Macmillan & Free Press, 1964)
Znaniecki, F. *The Social Role of the Man of Knowledge* (Octagon Books, New York, 1965) (first published 1940)

12 BIOGRAPHIC SKETCH AND BIBLIOGRAPHY OF LEO KUPER

Leo Kuper was born in Johannesburg on 24 November 1908. His parents were among the many Jews who emigrated from small towns in Eastern Europe to escape anti-Semitism during the Czarist regime. Leo, the second son and the youngest of five children, attended local English-medium government schools. After matriculating at the age of 15, he entered the University of Witwatersrand where he obtained an Honours degree in English, and in 1934 the LL B.

For the next eleven years he practiced as an attorney in Johannesburg; he also worked closely with Legal Aid, a group of trade unionists and African leaders active in improving living and labour conditions, and took part in interracial organisations. He was reading widely in political theory, literature, history and anthropology. In January 1935 he married Hilda Beemer, while she was doing anthropological field work in Swaziland. In the course of the following decades, Hilda Kuper became one of the leading anthropologists of her generation, and the exceptionally harmonious intellectual companionship between Leo and Hilda soon became a central element in both of their distinguished careers.

When Hitler invaded Poland, and Fascist and racist slogans were openly expressed in South Africa, Leo felt morally compelled to join the (voluntary) South African Army and its Western allies. It was a hard decision for someone who was reserved, sensitive, intellectually alert, opposed to physical violence; but he felt there was no alternative.

He enlisted as a private, was subsequently promoted to lieutenant and then captain, and, for two years, served outside of South Africa — in East Africa, Egypt and Italy. As an education officer, his duties included running literacy courses, producing a daily newssheet, and helping the men with legal advice. A few South African soldiers seeking some way to commemorate the victims of war and oppression agreed to try to establish 'a living war memorial'. They finally decided on community centres providing preventive health services for Africans. Leo was one of the founders and was largely responsible for organising and publicising its ideals. Publicity concentrated largely on exposing African living conditions and the tragic effects of racial discrimination on African health and infant mortality rates. After demobilisation Leo was appointed full-time secretary, but once the National War Memorial Health Foundation received official recognition, bureaucratisation and parliamentarianism blunted the message and diluted the idealism.

It had become clear to Leo that he did not want to return to legal practice nor be an administrator (though he was doing a superb job within the limits of the structure). At the age of 39, he decided to become a sociologist. On the recommendation of an American Labour Attache in Johannesburg, Leo applied to the University of North Carolina, where Rupert Vance and Howard Odum were teaching. In August 1947 Leo and Hilda Kuper left for the States, and in 1949 he obtained his MA. Though he was accepted at Chicago for his Doctorate, illness in the family brought him back temporarily to South Africa. He had no capital and no work and was glad when the University of Birmingham in England offered him a post as lecturer with the opportunity to work as a sociologist with a team of town planners. *Living in Towns* is one of the results of this study.

In 1952, he received his PhD from the University of Birmingham and was invited to take the chair of sociology at the University of Natal in Durban. The Kupers returned to South Africa with their two daughters, then three and two years old, and remained until 1961 (except for six months' leave in England attached to the University of Manchester). The Durban phase of his life is reflected in three major works: *Passive Resistance in South Africa; Durban: A Study of Racial Ecology;* and *An African Bourgeoisie*. *Passive Resistance* and *An African Bourgeoisie* (which won the Herskowitz Award of the African Studies Association) were banned in South Africa. A fourth book of the South African phase of Leo's career, *The College Brew*, is a satirical novel about 'Bantu Education', and proved an uncannily accurate prediction of the direction the Government-sponsored 'bush colleges' would take. His writing and his teaching were part of a philosophy expressed in his activities in the South African Liberal Party, in which Leo played a leading role.

In 1961 Leo became Professor in the Department of Sociology at the University of California at Los Angeles, and, though no longer directly involved in politics, continued in his teaching and in his writing to analyse conflicts and to seek ways of resolving them. His latest book, *The Pity of It All*, a comparative study of revolution in Algeria, Zanzibar, Burundi and Rwanda, is the most recent culmination of that work. In 1967 Leo became an American citizen, and in 1968 he was appointed Director of the African Studies Centre at UCLA (a tribute indeed to a former 'white South African'). He resigned the directorship in 1973, since he considered that the position of Director should circulate. His directorship covered five years of major campus turmoil, but his leadership and understanding won unqualified praise from students and faculty, and the Centre grew in strength and rating. Among the outstanding colloquia run by the Centre was the joint effort of Leo and M.G. Smith which resulted in *Pluralism in Africa*. The range of his publications appears in the bibliography; the humanist approach is evident in all. Though (or perhaps, because) Leo is not in the mainstream of American sociology, the quality and integrity of his work has received wide recognition. He has been invited to contribute to international conferences and is at present extending his research to Northern Ireland, in the spirit of the liberal tradition. In recognition of his life's work in the field of race relations, the American Sociological Association awarded him its Spivack Award in 1978.

Bibliography of Leo Kuper

Books

Living in Towns: Selected Research Papers in Urban Sociology (ed.) (The Cresset Press, London, 1953)

Passive Resistance in South Africa (Jonathan Cape, London, 1956; Yale University Press, 1957)

Durban: A Study in Racial Ecology, with Hilstan Watts and Ronald Davies, (Columbia University Press, New York, 1958)

The College Brew (a satire) (Universal Printing Works, Durban, 1960)

African Law: Adaptation and Development, with Hilda Kuper (eds.) (University of California Press, Berkeley and Los Angeles, 1965)

An African Bourgeoisie: Race, Class, and Politics in South Africa, (Yale University Press, New Haven, 1965 (Herskowitz Award))

Pluralism in Africa, with M.G. Smith (eds.) (University of California Press, Berkeley and Los Angeles, 1969)

Race, Class and Power (Duckworth and Co., London, 1974)

Race, Science and Society (ed.) (The UNESCO Press, Paris, and Columbia University Press, New York, 1975)

The Pity of It All (Duckworth and Co., London, 1977 and University of Minnesota Press, Minneapolis, 1977)

Articles

'The South African Native: Caste, Proletariat or Race?, *Social Forces* (1949), 28, 2, pp. 146-53

'Social Science Research and the Planning of Urban Neighborhoods', *Social Forces* (1951), 29, 3, pp. 237-43

'Some Demographic Aspects of White Supremacy in South Africa', *British Journal of Sociology* (1950), 1, 2, pp. 144-53

'The Background of Passive Resistance (South Africa, 1952)' (included in *Passive Resistance*), *British Journal of Sociology* (1953), 4, 3, pp. 243-56

'Blueprint for Living Together', in Leo Kuper (ed.), *Living in Towns* (Cresset Press, London, 1953), pp. 1-202
'The Control of Social Change: a South African Experiment', *Social Forces* (1954), 33, 1, pp. 19-29
'The Heightening of Racial Tension', *Race* (1960), 2, pp. 24-32
'Racialism and Integration in South African Society', *Race* (1963), 4, pp. 26-31
'The Problem of Violence in South Africa', *Inquiry* (1964), 7, pp. 295-303
'Sociological Aspects of Housing Discrimination', in John H. Denton (ed.), *Race and Property* (Diablo Press, Berkeley, 1964), pp. 122-233
'Religion and Urbanization in Africa', in J. Matthes (ed.), *Religious Pluralism and Social Structure, International Yearbook for the Sociology of Religion* (1965), I, pp. 213-33
'Sociology – some Aspects of Urban Plural Societies', in Robert A. Lystad (ed.), *The African World: A Survey of Social Research* (Praeger, New York, 1965), pp. 107-30
'South Africa's Experience in the Mismanagement of Race Relations', Conference on Law Enforcement and Racial and Cultural Tensions, October, 8-10, 1965 (University of California Extension and The School of Criminology, University of California, Berkeley, 1966) pp. 163-77
'Structural Discontinuities in African Towns: Some Aspects of Racial Pluralism', in Horace Miner (ed.), *The City in Modern Africa* (Pall Mall Press, London and Praeger, New York, 1967), pp. 127-50
'The Political Situation of Non-Whites in South Africa', in William Hance, Leo Kuper, Vernon McKay, and Edwin S. Munger (eds.), *Southern Africa and the United States* (Columbia University Press, New York, 1968), pp. 65-104
'Segregation', *International Encyclopedia of the Social Sciences*, 14, edited by David L. Sills (Macmillan and The Free Press, 1968), pp. 144-50
'Non-Violence Revisited', in R. Rotberg and A. Mazrui (eds.), *Protest and Power in Black Africa* (Oxford University Press, 1970), pp. 788-804
'Race Structure in the Social Consciousness', *Civilisations* (1970), 20, 1, pp. 88-103
'African Nationalism', in Monica Wilson and Leonard Thompson (eds.), *Cambridge History of South Africa*, vol. II (international edition only) (Clarendon Press, London, 1971), pp. 424-75
'Continuities and Discontinuities in Race Relations: Evolutionary or Revolutionary Change', *Cahiers d'Etudes Africaines* (1970), 10, 3, pp. 361-83
'Stratification in Plural Societies: Focus on White Settler Societies in Africa', in Leonard Plotnicov and Arthur Tuden (eds.), *Essays in Comparative Social Stratification* (University of Pittsburgh Press, Pittsburgh, 1970), pp. 77-94
"Theories of Revolution in Race Relations', *Comparative Studies in Society and History* (1971), 13,1, pp. 87-107
'Class and Colour in South Africa – 1850-1950: Some Problems in Marxism and Pluralism' (review article) (April 1971), *Race*, pp. 495-500
'Ideologies of Violence among Subordinate Groups', *Transactions of the Sixth World Congress of Sociology* (1970), III, pp. 225-40
'Race, Class and Power: Some Comments on Revolutionary Change', *Comparative Studies in Society and History* (1972), 14, pp. 400-21
'Political Change in Plural Societies: Problems in Racial Pluralism', *International Social Science Journal* (1971), XXIII, pp. 594-604
A Recorded Talk for Open University, BBC – 'Non-Violence as Political Action', April 1973
'On Theories of Race Relations', introductory chapter in Bell and Freeman, *Ethnicity and Nation Building* (Sage Publications, 1974)

NOTES ON CONTRIBUTORS

Heribert Adam, a German-born Canadian, is Professor of Sociology at Simon Fraser University in Canada, and the author of numerous publications on South Africa, especially *Modernizing Racial Domination*, and *South Africa, Sociological Perspectives*.

Edna Bonacich, an American raised in South Africa, is Associate Professor of Sociology at the University of California, Riverside, and a specialist in race and ethnic relations. She authored several articles on middleman minorities and the split labour market.

Hamish Dickie-Clark, a South African who emigrated to Canada, is Professor of Sociology at Simon Fraser University, Canada. He is the author of a study of Coloureds in South Africa, *The Marginal Situation*, and a number of articles.

Adam Kuper, a South African, is Professor of Anthropology and African Studies at the University of Leiden, The Netherlands. The author of several books, his main piece of Southern African scholarship is *Kalahari Village Politics*.

Hilda Kuper, born in Zimbabwe and a Swazi citizen, is Professor Emeritus of Anthropology at the University of California in Los Angeles. Among her numerous Southern African publications are *An African Aristocracy, Indian People in Natal, The Swazi, The Uniform of Colour*, and *Sobhuza II*.

Fatima Meer, a South African, is Senior Lecturer in Sociology at the University of Natal, Durban, and was repeatedly arrested and persecuted for her political activities. She has published extensively on South Africans of Indian origin, and her main work is titled *Race and Suicide in South Africa*.

Kogila A. Moodley, a South African emigre to Canada, is Assistant Professor of Anthropology at the University of British Columbia. Her South African work focused on academic apartheid.

Notes on Contributors

Margo Russell, a South African sociologist, is Lecturer at the University of East Anglia. Her research has dealt with residential segregation in South Africa, and the Afrikaner farming community in the Kalahari. Her most recent book is entitled *Afrikaners of the Kalahari*.

Pierre L. van den Berghe, an American citizen born in Zaire of Franco-Belgian ancestry, is Professor of Sociology and Anthropology at the University of Washington. His books on South Africa include *South Africa, A Study in Conflict*, and *Caneville*.

Hilstan L. Watts, a South African, is Professor of Sociology at the University of Natal, Durban. His main field is urban ecology, and he co-authored with Leo Kuper the book, *Durban, A study in Racial Ecology*.

INDEX

Academic Freedom Committees (Cape Town, Witwatersrand) 28, 119, 131
Adam, K. 118, 125, 131
African Bourgeoisie, An (Kuper) 43, 154
African National Congress (ANC) 23, 31-5, 49, 50, 57, 60, 100, 139, 147, Youth League 57; – Resistance Movement 35
'Africanisation' 118, 127, 129, Jackson Commission on 126
Algeria 10, 15, 16, 44, 45, 58, 61, 154
America, Latin 15; – North 16, 20, 24
Angola 16, 45
anti-Semitism 41, 153
apartheid *passim*; cost of 62-3; legislative basis of 31-3
Arblaster, A. 51, 54
Arens, W. 95
Association for the Educational and Cultural Advancement of the African 101
Atmore, Anthony 38-9
Australia 16, 62, 109, 110, 114

Ballinger, Margaret 33, 46
banning 18, 23, 28n3, 33, 36, 43, 74, 99-100, 125, 136, 139, 150n3, *see also* censorship
Bantu Prophets in South Africa (Sundkler) 82
Bantustans/'homelands' 110, 128
Barash, David 58, 66
Beals, Ralph L. 28
Becker, Howard and Barnes, Harry E. 70, 76
Beidelman, T.O. 95
Biko, Steve 100
Binsbergen, W.M.J. van 88, 94n, 95
Black Community Programme 125, 131; – Unity Front 100
Blanchet-Cohen, T. 95
Blank, Joost de 9
Blumer, Herbert 39, 46
Bonacich, Edna 12, 106-16, 157
Boshoff, Prof. 130n7

Botha 50
Botswana 84-90, Bechuanaland 138
boycotts 13, 49, 50, 57, university 20, 123-6, 128, 144
Brandel-Syrier, M. 104
Britain 8, 10, 12, 16, 20, 30-1, 36, 51, 113
Brookes, Edgar H. 9, 21, 28, 40
Brown, J.T. 87, 95
Brown, Peter 9, 33
Bureau of Racial Affairs, South African 10, 138, 142, 151n7
Burger, Die 151n5
Burundi 45, 58, 154
Buthelezi, Chief Gatsha 100, 128

Calvinism 7
Campaign against Unjust Laws 139
Camus, Albert 44, 46
Canada 16, 28n5, 62, 157
Cape Times 125, 132
capitalism 15-16, 36-7, 39, 61, 63, 68-9, 71-2, 107-16
Carter, G., Karis, T. and Stulz, M. 150n2, 152
Casalis, Rev. E. 77, 95
caste 73, 109, 110
censorship 9, 20, 28n2, 43, 46n9, 71, 74, 136, 150n3,4
censuses 97-9, 104, 105
Christian Institute 36
Christianity 30, 46n5, 69-72, 75, 77-96, 142, 151n8; black 77, 79-90, *see also* Independent churches, Protestantism 69, 71, 94
churches, 90, Anglican, Roman Catholic 61; Dutch Reformed 61, 91, 93; Independent 80-90, 91, 93, *see also* missionaries; religion
class 8, 12, 35, 59, 63-5, 73, struggle 107-16
Class and Colour in South Africa (H.J. and R.E. Simons) 40
Colenso, Bishop 79
College Brew, The (Kuper) 117, 154, 155

colonialism 7-8, 12, 56, 113, 138
Coloureds 56, 60, 98, 104n1, 107, 115, 118, 119, 130n1,5, 138, 139, 157; Congress 139
Commissions, Holloway 138; International Jurists 150n1; Jackson 126; Snyman 126-7
communism 24-5, 31, 33, 34, 35, 40-1, 46n3, 50, 52, 64; Suppression of Communism Act (1950) 31, 34, 43, 100, 136, 139, 150n3,4, 151n16
Communist Party 35, 40, 57, 59
community activity 28n5, 99-104, 121, 129
Comte, Auguste 68, 70-2
Congress, Alliance 57; movement 11, 12, 14; of Democrats 50, 57, 63; of the People 34, 139, *see also* African National, Coloured, Indians, Pan-African
consciousness, black 21-2, 99-100, 123, 135; white 22
Contact 34

Dachs, J.A. 95
Dahrendorf, Ralf 25-6, 28
Daily Dispatch 125, 132
Danziger, K. 133, 152
De Kiewiet, Cornelis 9
Deloria, Vine Jr. 69, 76
Desmond, Cosmas 28n3
Dickie-Clark, Hamish 27n1, 48-55, 157
Dixon, Keith 54
Driver 20
Durban: A Study of Racial Ecology (Kuper) 154, 155
Durkheim, E. 73, 87, 95
Dutch East India Co. 108

economics 14-16, 36, 61-2
education 11, 27, 33, 113, 118, 120-1, 139; Bantu 45, 154, – Education Act (1953) 31, 139, – *Education Journal* 151n9, *see also* universities
emigration, white 16, 56, 62, 66n5
employment 64, 97-9, 107-16, *see also* labour
Erikson 52, 54
Ethiopia 14, 91
Europe, Eastern 18, 153; Western 14, 24, 36
exile 9, 19-20

Fanon, Franz 10, 23, 28, 46n10
Fiat Lux 122, 132
France 10, 16, 25, 36
franchise, extension of 30-1, 49, 50, 138
Freedom Charter 28n4, 34, 35
Frelimo 126
Freud, Sigmund 54, 72

Galtung 27
Gandhi, Mahatma 12, 14, 56; Gandhism 8-10, 57, 60
genetics 58-9
Gerhart, G.M. 131
Germany, Nazi 10, 17, 24
Ghana 10, 138
Gluckman, Max 9, 46
Gordimer, Nadine 9
Gouldner, Alvin W. 17, 22, 28
Graphic, The 127, 132
Green, T. H. 53-4
Group Areas Act (1950) 31, 32, 136

Habermas, Jurgen 17, 28
Hampden-Turner, C.M. 46
health 27, 153; National War Memorial Health Foundation 154
Herskowitz Award 43, 154
Hinduism 69, 72, 75, 84
Hobhouse, L.T. 45n2, 46
Hoernlé, R.F.A. 31, 46, 48, 49
Holland 10, 36, 157
Hoover, K.R. 51-4
Horrell, Muriel 119, 125-8, 130n1,4, 131, 137-46, 152; and Horner, D. and Hudson, J. 143, 145, 152
Horton, R. 83, 95
Horwitz, Ralph 9
housing 27
Huddleston, Trevor 9
humanism 30-2; African 32
Hunter, Monica 46
Hurley, Denis 9
Hugo, A. 151n5

ideology 7, 16, 26-7, 57, 80, 135; Afrikaner 26, 31, 75, 94; liberal 36, 39, 59-60, 63, 65; Marxist 8
immigration 109, 112-4
Immorality Amendment Act (1950) 31
Index of Objectionable Literature

Index

(Jacobsen) 150n3
India 10, 12, 14
Indians 33, 36, 56, 60, 64, 104n1, 107, 115, 117, 130n1,3, 131n10,11, 138, 157; Congress 56, 139, Natal Congress 123, – Organisation 56; 'Indianisation' 118, 120, 129; university *see* universities, Durban-Westville
'Inkatha Yen-Kululeko Yesizwe Ka Zulu' 100,
Institute of Race Relations, South African 36, 123, 131, 138-9, 152
intellectuals, definition of 133-5; role of 8-11, 13, 17-28, 30-47, 115, 133-52
Internal Security Act (1976) 100, 150n4
Ireland, Northern 155
Ireland, R.R. 120, 131
Islam 69, 75
Ivory Coast 61

Jacobsen 150n3
Japan 14
job reservation/segration 109-11, *see also* labour
Judaism 30, 32, 75, 83

Kadalie, Clements 40
Kahl, Joseph A. 70, 76
Kalahari 84-90, 157, 158
Katchipaha 86, 88, 89
Keesings Contemporary Archives 151n4,16
Kenya 61, 138
Khoapa, Bennie 100
Kiernan, J.P. 95
Kovaly, Pavel 37, 46
Krige, E.J. 80, 95
Kuper, Adam 77-96, 157
Kuper, Hilda 9, 13, 30-47, 80, 91-2, 153-5, 157
Kuper, Leo 9, 11-14, 17, 20-1, 23, 27, 28, 31, 43-8, 55, 58, 59, 74, 81, 83, 91, 94, 100, 104, 106, 111, 116, 117, 130, 136, 139, 152, 153-6, 158; and Smith M.G. 45n1, 106, 116, 155

labour, displacement 64, 108-12; market, split 62, 106-16; migrant 107, 113
Langa 34

Language, F.J. 95n6, 96
Laslett, Barbara 116
Leader, The 122, 123, 131n8, 132
Legassick, M. and Shingler, J. 140, 146, 147, 152
Lerner, Max 47
Lewin, Julius 9
Lewis, Ethelreda 40
Lewsen, P. 47
Liberal Party 11, 13, 39, 40, 9 49, 56, 59, 66n4, 122, 138, 154; and African Congresses 33-6, 57, 60; and English business 63-4; and Indians 60
liberalism *passim*; Cape 8, 30-1, 49-50, 63; definition of 11-12, 49; failure of 8, 21-3, 48-51, 56-67; misrepresentation of 37-41, 46n7; philosophy of 30-2, 36, 51-4, 56, 59-61, *see also* ideology, Liberal Party
Lipset, S.M. 36, 47, 134, 152; and Ladd, E.C. 134, 148, 150, 151n17
Living in Towns (Kuper) 154, 155
Livingstone, David 77-9, 84, 85, 90, 91, 94n1, 86
Luthuli, Chief Albert 9, 31, 32, 34, 45, 46n5, 47, 57

M.L. Sultan Technical College 125
Mackenzie, J. 77, 95n4, 96
Macmillan, W.M. 95n3, 96
Mafeje, Archie 9, 80, 96, 146
magic 77-96
Malherbe, E.G. 9
Mandela, Nelson 35, 47
Mannheim, Karl 22, 29, 133
Marcum, John 19-20, 29
Marquard, Leo 9, 21, 29, 66
Marxism/Marxists 7, 8, 11-12, 22, 24, 35, 40, 50, 51, 63, 64, 80, 113, 135, 147, 151n12
Mathews, Z.K. 9, 21, 57
Mayer, P. 80, 96
Mbanjwa, T. 120, 124, 126, 136
Mdlalose, Dr Frank 100
Mead 54
medicine 11, 27, 97-105; African 78-9, 87, 89
Meer, Fatima 9, 11, 14, 68-76, 131, 151n4, 157
Mexico 15, 109, 112
missionaries 32, 50, 77-96; and education 32, 50, 57, 146;

and politics 79-81; London Missionary Society 79, 85, 88, 89, 91
Mngadi, Elliott 33
Modernizing Racial Domination (Adam) 41
Modisane, Blake 9
Moffat, R. 79, 85, 95n2, 96
Mokitimi, Rev. 83
Moodley, Kogila A. 27n1, 117-32, 157
Moore, Barrington 24, 29
Moroka, Dr James 100
Mozambique 16, 45, 126
Mphahlele, Ezekiel 9
Msimang, H. Selby 40

Naicker, G.M. 123
Namibia 63
Natal Mercury 123
nationalisation 11, 33, 39
nationalism 51-2, 141; Afrikaner 7, 31, 49, 50, 163; black 7-8, 25, 49, 50, 57, 65, 129, 141
Nationalist Party, Afrikaner 31, 33, 40, 60, 137
Naude, Beyers 9
Nettl, J. P. 17, 29, 133, 135, 148, 152
Nettleton, Clive 22, 29
New Zealand 16, 62
Ngubane, Dr Baldwin 100
Ngubane, Jordan 9
Nicolaus, Martin 72, 76
Nietzche 24
Nkonyane, Bishop 90
Nkrumah 10
Non-European Unity Movement 146
non-violence 12-13, 23-4, 36, 49, 60, 106; Non-Violent Resistance Campaign 32-3
Nyembezi, Dr Hugo 100

Odum, Howard 154
Oxford History of South Africa 38-9, 46n9

Pan-African Congress 34, 57, 147
Parsons, Talcott 71, 72, 76, 134, 152
Pass laws 32, 34, 135
Passive Resistance in South Africa (Kuper) 12, 43, 154, 155
paternalism 7-8, 21, 33, 66n3, 112, 121-3, 126, 135
Paton, Alan 9, 21, 24, 29, 46n6, 66

Pauw, B.A. 83, 86, 87, 91, 96, 104
Piek, Ben 25
Pityana, N. 100
Pity of All, The (Kuper) 14, 45, 154
Pluralism in Africa (Kuper and Smith) 155
Population Registration Act (1950) 31
Portugal 16
poverty 74-5; Datum Line 75, *see also* Labour, wages
Progressive Party 28n4, 49, 56, 63, 122
Prohibition of Improper Interference Act (1968) 36
Prohibition of Mixed Marriages Act (1949) 31
propaganda 40, 43, 112-3
protectionism 112-3
Publications Control Board 150n3

Race 38, 46
Ramfol, Prof. 120
Ranchod, Prof. 124
Rand Daily Mail 130n7, 132
Rand Revolt (1922) 110
Reality 21
Reddy, Govin 123
Reeves, Ambrose 9
reform, constitutional 21; land 11, 15, 33, 39, 64; political 26-7, 28n4, 36, 80
Rehumanization or Dehumanization? (Kovaly) 37
religion 32, 77-96, 103, 142; African 32, 77-9, 86-7, 89-90, 92-3
research, academic 19, 24, 27
Reservation of Separate Amenit Amenities Act (1953) 139
Return to Laughter 9
revolution 8, 10, 13, 15-16, 58, 65, 113-14
Rhodesia 16, 45, 62, 66n5, 100
Riesman, David 47
Riotous Assemblies Act (1956) 40, 126
Rivonia trial 35
Robertson, Janet 34, 46n6, 47, 48, 66
Robertson-Smith, W. 87, 96
Russell, Margo 133-52, 158
Rwanda 45, 58, 154

sabotage 13, 35, 147-8
satyagraha 12

Index

Schapera, Isaac 9, 78-80, 86, 87, 90, 94n1, 95n6, 96
Schapiro, J.S. 45n2, 47
Schmidt, J.J. 97, 105
Schutte, A.G. 91, 96
Sechele, Chief 77-9
Seme, P. Ka I. 32, 46n5
Separate Representation of Voters Act 32
Sharpeville 34, 61
Shaw, Martin 74, 76
Shils, Edward 24, 29, 134, 148, 152
Simmel, Georg 52-3, 54n1, 55
Simons, H.J. and R.E. 40, 71
Simons, Jack 9
Skinner 52, 54
Smuts, Jan 9, 50
Sobhuza, King 90-1
socialism 8, 11, 24, 59, 65, 113-5; and liberalism 51-3
sociobiology 58-9, 66n2,3
sociology/social sciences 11, 13, 19, 24, 25, 42, 68-76, 106, 154-5, *see also* University of Natal, Sociology Department
South Africa and the Rule of Law (International Commission of Jurists) 150n1
Soviet Union 17, 22
Soweto rising 45, 125, 127-8, 149
Spear of the Nation (Unkhonto we Sizwe Sizwe) 35
Springfield Teachers Training College 125
SPROCAS 29
Star, The 25, 127, 132
Stock Limitation Acts 32
strikes 13, 34, 128
students 23, 117-31, 133, 151n4; African Students Association, – Union of South Africa 147; National Union of South African Students (Nusas) 18, 20, 23, 36, 123, 138, 139-40, 146; South African Students Organisation (SASO) 99, 123, 125, 127, 147, 149; Student Representative Councils (SRCs) 122-6, 151n14
Sunday Express 125, 132; – *Times* 123, 132; – *Tribune* 124, 132
Sundkler, B. 80, 82-4, 91, 93, 96
Suzman, Helen 9
Swaziland 80, 90-2

Terrorism Act 128
Thompson, Leonard 9
Times, The (London) 144, 150n3
Tiro, O. R. 125
trade unions 23, 27, 36-7, 40, 109; Industrial and Commercial Union 40; Tucsa 23
treason 34, 35, 71
Tristes Tropiques 9

Uganda 60
United Party 28n4, 33, 49, 60, 63
United States 10, 16, 62, 66n3, 109, 112; civil rights movement 15
Unity Movement 63
universities 17-28, 117-52; Afrikaans 17, 129, 133, 136, 142; autonomy of 17-18, 65, 118, 126, 137, 139-46, 148, 151n7,15, University Amendment Act (1968) 151n15; black 17-19, 25, 75, 117-32, 137-45; 'open' English-language 17-20, 26, 119, 120, 123, 128, 136, 137, 139-40, 145, Open Universities Liaison Committee 140; politicisation of 17, 26-7, 28n5, 117-32, 146-9; racial segregation in 117-32, 137-46, Extension of University Education Bill/Act (1959) 130n1, 141, 143, 145, Separate University Education Bill (1957) 138, 140-1
University, Birmingham 154, British Columbia 157; California 14, 45, 154, 157; Cape Town 28, 74, 99, 130n1, 131, 137, 140, 145-6, 151n16; College of the North, Turfloop 125, 126, 130n7, 143, 149, College for Indians, Durban-Westville 19, 118-26, 127, 128, 130n4, 130n4,5, 131n8,9; East Anglia 158; Fort Hare 127, 137-8, 140-1, 143, 149, 150, – Transfer Act (1959) 141, 143; Leiden 157; London 119; Manchester 154; Natal 27n1, 43, 100, 118, 130n1, 138, 139, 140, 143, 145, 151n14,16, black medical school 97, 99, 104n1, 127, 137, 140, Sociology Department 13-14, 74, 117, 154, 157, 158; Potchefstrom 9, 138, 142, 145, 149-50, 151n7; Pretoria 9, 75, 99, 146; Rand Afrikaans 25,

146; Rhodes 74, 137, 140; South Africa 119, 121; Stellenbosch 9, 75, 146, 151n5; Washington 158; the Western Cape, Kasselsvlei 125, 127-8, 143, 149; the Witwatersrand 28, 99, 130n1, 131, 137, 139-40, 145-6, 153;Zululand, Ngoya 127, 128, 143, 149

van den Berghe, Pierre L. 7-16, 18, 19, 21, 29, 56-67, 74, 116, 158
van der Walt, Prof. 122
Vance, Rupert 154
Verwoerd, H.F. 9, 75, 117, 142
violence 12-13, 14, 23-4, 45, 46n6, 50, 56, 58-9
Vorster, John 63

wage rates 39, 40, 62, 107-16
Wallerstein, Immanuel 27, 29
Walshe, P. 131
Walzer, Michael 47

Watts, Hilstan L. 97-105, 158
Weber, Max 17, 29, 47
welfare services 11, 33, 37; legislation 109
Welsh, David 19, 29
West, M. 82, 91, 96
Westlake, Nancy 38-9
Willoughby, W.C. 86, 95n4, 96
Wilson, Edward O. 58, 67
Wilson, Monica 9
Wilson, R. 82-4, 96
Wolff, Kurt 53, 55
World, The 125, 132
World University Service 119
World War II 8, 12, 63, 153
Wright Mills, C. 41, 47

Xuma, A.B. 32, 57, 100

Zaire 158
Zansibar 45, 58, 154
Zimbabwe 15, 63
Znaniecki, F. 134, 152

For Product Safety Concerns and Information please contact our EU representative GPSR@taylorandfrancis.com
Taylor & Francis Verlag GmbH, Kaufingerstraße 24, 80331 München, Germany

www.ingramcontent.com/pod-product-compliance
Lightning Source LLC
Chambersburg PA
CBHW070618300426
44113CB00010B/1579